RIDERS OF THE COSMIC C...

Rajneesh is an enigma. Despite ridicule in the popular press, he has drawn thousands of Westerners into his following. What lies at the heart of the magnetic appeal which draws people to the leading gurus?

Tal Brooke shows that their essence is not a new teaching but a new consciousness. Rajneesh, Sai Baba, Muktananda – each has undergone a mind-blowing explosion into a new mode of being. Just what is this 'superconsciousness' and what does it lead to? → evil !

The author, Tal Brooke, has held a privileged position in the inner circle of Sai Baba devotees in India. This experience also helped him gain the confidence of members of the Rajneesh ashram in India. His account of these three leading gurus draws some fascinating conclusions.

Son of American diplomat parents, Tal Brooke grew up in Europe and the Middle East. His book on Sai Baba, *Avatar of Night*, has been a bestseller in India. He has spoken widely at British and American universities, and was the subject of a CBN feature on US television.

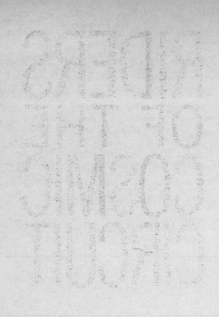

RIDERS
OF THE
COSMIC
CIRCUIT

TAL BROOKE

RESEARCH BY JOHN WELDON

A LION PAPERBACK
Tring · Batavia · Sydney

Acknowledgment

Along with John Weldon who helped me with research, I would like gratefully to
acknowledge the aid of a few dear friends who contributed in different ways
towards this book. They include: The entire Hedrick family, especially OD,
Charles and Vikke Jarvis, Dr Anthony and Cynthia Morton, Dr Preston
Campbell (and Elaine), George and Dreena Verwer (who have distributed some
of my books in numerous countries), Horizon School, Ron and Angel Jolivette,
and finally Ed (and Ruth) Nutter who loaned me an Apple computer and taught
me how to use it (which involved midnight bail-outs when bytes seemed frozen in
the inner core of computer memory). And finally I would like to thank my father,
Edgar Brooke, who provided sound editorial insight and warm encouragement.

Published by
Lion Publishing plc
Icknield Way, Tring, Herts, England
ISBN 0 7459 1217 6
Lion Publishing Corporation
1705 Hubbard Avenue, Batavia, Illinois 60510, USA
ISBN 0 7459 1217 6
Albatross Books Pty Ltd
PO Box 320, Sutherland, NSW 2232, Australia
ISBN 0 86760 860 9

First edition 1986
Reprinted 1987

British Library Cataloguing in Publication Data

Brooke, Tal
  Riders of the cosmic circuit.
  1. Mysticism——India
  I. Title
  291.4'2   BL625
  ISBN 0 7459 1217 6

Printed in Great Britain
by Cox & Wyman, Reading

CONTENTS

PART I

THE EXPLOSION
PERSPECTIVE ONE

SAI BABA

MUKTANANDA

RAJNEESH

PART II

THE EXPLOSION
PERSPECTIVE TWO

Preface

The Riders of the Cosmic Circuit are possibly the most exclusive, powerful, and secretive of inner-circles in existence. To get on the inside requires the most prized initiation conceivable. And only a fraction of humanity ever appears at that rarefied level of adeptship required even to attempt the radical journey in consciousness. The opening bid is to offer with total abandon one's soul on the altar of oblivion. The goal is an Explosion of super-consciousness beyond the point of no return. What emerges from this transformation is an Enlightened Master who claims to be nothing less than God using a physical body as a medium.

Most Riders of the Cosmic Circuit are from the East. Yet today several adepts from the West are waiting in the wings for this Explosion. In twenty years the Riders have changed the contours of this world more than we know. And their advent, some say, has only begun. For the Grand Design is to initiate humanity into the Dawn of a New Age—for which countless advocates await the advent of these masters, gods, and supermen who are to be the catalysts. The behind-the-scenes footwork in preparation for this planned global shift in consciousness has been staggering.

An ancient tradition has long declared that there are only two perspectives of this Explosion into super-consciousness that no one but a Rider can go through. On the outside, from where the world tries to peer in, there is only a fathomless void, like a black hole, which sucks in all light and reflects not even a photon back. The only clues available are the before and after transformations of the person, and the baffling experiences, claims, and revelations coming from those who have crossed the gulf. This perspective is taken in this book's first part.

The other perspective is from the inside of the Explosion, reserved only for those who have crossed the infinite gulf and who now peer out into our mode of existence and reality from a totally alien and unreachable perspective. Or so we are told.

We are left with a totally unsolvable paradox. How can one who is not a Rider reach this state of consciousness while remaining human enough to smuggle back the secret? Who can pass through the ultimate initiation beyond the point of no return, where the Ride begins, to get around the paradox? No one, we are told. We are left in a seller's market—only those who know can ever know . . . and their claim stands alone as the final authority never to be resolved *a priori*. That's what they say . . . Or is there yet another perspective?

PART I
—THE EXPLOSION—
PERSPECTIVE ONE

1

SAI BABA
INDIA'S ONLY AVATAR

'*He is God in human form, now on earth for the first time in many many centuries.*' Such were the winsome words of the tall and stunning New Delhi girl, beaming at me from under her sun umbrella not far from the Gandhi Memorial.

They went to my heart, these words. Then, uncannily, that afternoon I opened up *Newsweek* magazine there in Delhi, and the main feature in the 'religion' section was about 'India's first Avatar since Krishna'. Rather than turn water into wine, as Christ did at Cana, this God-on-earth turned water into gasoline in the desert wilderness of Andhra Pradesh. The occasion? His car had run out of gasoline. So he directed the local villagers to fetch water out of the well, and before their gasping faces, he touched it, and as it was poured into his tank the smell of gasoline wafted everywhere. He drove off before an awed crowd of South Indians. He was famous for accounts such as these, as numberless as saffron petals on the mountains of Kashmir.

Who was this God-man that I had just heard about? His name was Sai Baba!

Both sources (the New Delhi girl and *Newsweek*) seemed to be speaking to me, I felt, from above the realm of coincidence. Such unexpected news in full synchronicity appeared to be a sort of telegram from the cosmic gate-keeper. Here was my cue. The moment I had long awaited and the very reason I had come to India—to find One who had crossed the gulf of eternity and peered into the heart and secrets of all existence. If you will, a Rider of The Cosmic Circuit. One who has mastered the cosmos.

I sped across the Indian subcontinent on a train, detecting en route clusters of 'happenings' and omens that again seemed to go beyond coincidence. Events often seemed to communicate and answer needs, resembling a hidden presence guiding my steps, rather as a tin soldier is moved about a miniature battlefield. What manner of omens? A Mercedes Benz stops in front of the Madras railway station as I emerge. I am invited in. The ignition key chain has a picture of Sai Baba. The man driving is the only human being in Madras who knows exactly where Sai Baba is. He is the president of the Madras Sai Baba Seva Dal. I have been in Madras no more than ten minutes. I am graciously given specific directions with the parting words,

'Bhagavan is bringing you into his august presence, be assured'.

In a small town in Andhra Pradesh, I stand among Baba's elect devotees waiting for the arrival of his limousine. The hush spreads over the crowd. I am in the inner courtyard, where few are permitted. It has been over a month since I first got the news of Baba in Delhi.

Then a limousine glides into the gate through awed silence. Two dazzling eyes pierce the windshield. Baba emerges, as people stand at a respectful distance. He looks off into mountains and at the sky. His hands weave the air in cryptic gestures. The earth seems to stand still.

Sai Baba glows red in the coral-amber penumbra of South India's equatorial sunset. The door of his limousine is closed behind him. Before me undoubtedly stands the most magnetic human form I have ever seen in my life. The eyes remind me of a searching lighthouse.

Then my mood suddenly repolarizes by Baba's force, as I feel the contradiction that comes from being head-on with a presence superhumanly great. I am dwarfed. I feel hope and I feel the abyss. I am a clear-glass tumbler standing before an all-seeing-eye.

As devotees flow in a circular pattern around Baba, I see that I am not the only one who has felt his dynamo effect. Unlike every other Indian holy man I had visited, Baba did not project a thanatopic serenity or an austere severity. Baba is incredibly youthful, fresh like a spring flower, and has the vibrant energy of a bee.

I had been studying Baba's physical structure. Six inches shorter than the man he was standing before, or for that matter than any Indian there, he resembled a dwarf-sized giant. His huge head of wiry black hair flowed above a neck thick and muscular enough to have been transplanted from Bronco Nagurski of the Chicago Bears. Underneath this floating head was a diminutive, well-muscled little body narrowing down to two tiny feet. The whole was cloaked from neck to foot in a brilliant red robe, which made Baba's head appear to hover over an eternally frozen fiery jet of red flame.

Then I felt a second jolt as I saw Baba talking to an Indian near his car whose arms remained held up in a prayerful gesture. The Indian had made some kind of request, which Baba had already known about, telling the devotee the problem before he could even get the words out, in a quick, musical, raspy voice.

As the devotee's mouth dropped in awe, something else happened. Suddenly the flame color of Baba's robe flickered as Baba pulled up his sleeve. In an abracadabra motion he spun his arm in circles with the open palm down. My eyes bulged as I noticed suddenly that the hand was no longer empty. Thunderous electric waves, now covered in silence, seemed to pierce the air. Baba had worked a miracle! From nowhere he now held a handful of grey powder that he was pouring into the devotee's hand, instructing him to eat it. While the shaking devotee jibbered a thank you, Baba swivelled round flashing me a large sparkling smile. Before I could even react, he was busy talking to another man, explaining the man's personal family problems before the devotee even had a chance to tell them to Baba.

There was an immediately obvious non-human quality about Baba, but I was not sure I could define it. All that I could conclude was that 'non-human' suggested 'super' rather than 'sub' humanness, and only a 'full master' could transcend the human condition. As Baba proceeded from person to person, he seemed to act in absolute spontaneity, suggesting the busy impersonality of a bee vibrating pollen out of a flower. And this rebounding from person to person made me ponder a key idea of Vedanta—Baba's instant, spontaneous access to people's thoughts could only be explained by the concept of 'thoughtless-all-knowing'. Only an enlightened person without the limiting ego could harbor the infinite impersonal mind of God, as the mystics explain it. And this implied to me that Baba was like a walking doorway into the Absolute. When he talked or acted, it was merely the meeting-point of the impersonal godhead tuning down the cosmic wave-band to the comprehensible personal aspect of deity.

Baba suddenly spun away from the people he was talking to and came straight over to me. I reminded myself not to blow it by losing my poise.

Baba's English was practically baby-talk, while his black eyes told an entirely different story, radiating vibrant awareness. He did not seem to assess me, because he already knew me. 'Hello, Rowdeeee,' he chimed with taunting playfulness. Then looking concerned he asked,

'What's wrong, some sickness in the stomach?'

Baba was right. I had dysentery. I made a signal with my eyes to his hand as though to ask what he had been materializing. Baba anticipated the question.

'Oh yes . . . called *vibhuti*, divine ash.'

Again Baba's hand began rotating in wide circles for at least the fourth time in five minutes. In an instant he had a handful of grey powder sitting in his hand, which he immediately poured into mine saying,

'Eat, eat, it is good for the health.'

Static seemed to surge down the acrylic fiber of my shirt.

I stood there stunned eating the ash out of my hand. What I wanted to do, far from eating the ash, was to enshrine it in a glass case in the British Museum or take it to the Lawrence Berkeley radiation labs for analysis. I had seen a miracle! I was now eating that miracle! Yet I had in my hand the very evidence that would cut through the foundational philosophies that my culture was now so enamored with—the materialism, scientific pre-suppositions, indeed the empty logical positivism of our day and our institutions. There it was in my hand, a supernatural state-ment against all this empty-headed presumption. A telegram from the supernatural.

Before a silent crowd of onlookers, Baba looked me up and down. He patted me on the back.

'I have been waiting for you. It was I who made you come to India. You are near and dear.'

He seemed to know me better than my parents or a best friend. He also knew who I was. Later he would tell me he knew me in other lives, long before I was born in this life. Indeed he would tell me that I could not possibly have come into his presence had I not been very, very advanced spiritually in other lives. I was what mystics call an 'Adept'.

Later the next day I got a long private interview with Baba— the first of a great many—for which an Indian devotee will wait prayerfully for ten years. And only the closest ones even get such an interview. Baba stunned me by hugging me like a long lost son after materializing a robin's-egg-sized piece of rock sugar for me to eat. Then he described a mystical experience I had had out under the stars of the Virginia mountains one spring night while under a titanic dosage of LSD-25. That too he caused to happen.

'It was a taste, sir, of Samadhi, Nirvikalpa Samadhi, oneness with God. But only a taste, bas.'

He often called such things his 'calling cards'.

By the end of two years in India with Baba, I had lived in his house in Brindavan, spoken to groups of over twenty thousand on his ashram while up on stage with him, met a wide range of VIPs on Baba's behalf, published numerous works distributed around India, while being included in his inner circle. Some incredible things were destined to take place. More than I ever bargained for. But then Sai Baba claimed to be the world's only living avatar. Indeed, as he said time and again, the only avatar on earth for thousands of years.

What is an avatar? An avatar is God willing himself into birth. According to the Hindus, God never lived as an ordinary mortal, reincarnating to higher levels and ultimately self-perfecting. An avatar, like Krishna, breaks out of the ocean of Brahman to enter the earth to change one age to another age. This age, the Indian Puranas say, is the Kali Yuga, the age of iron and wickedness, and Vishnu will appear this time as Kalki, the final avatar.

Sai Baba has claimed since the time he was a boy that he is the Kalki Avatar (as well as the returned Christ). He is the only one alive in India purporting to work great miracles. He also has a following now in excess of twenty million dedicated devotees, if not hundreds of millions of general devotees. Sai Baba is the only one ever in India to live and have temples built where people come to worship him during his lifetime. In India, it is only after a God-man passes away that they erect a shrine to him. That was

15

true with Ramakrishna, Ramanah Maharshi, and Chaitanya.

Comparing an Avatar to an Enlightened yogi, Swami, or Maharishi is, to the Indians, like comparing a Maharajah to a cloth merchant in a shanti. Yogis like Marharishi Mahesh Yogi or Swamis like Chinmayananda have been known to come to Sai Baba for his blessings. Baba goes to no one for their endorsement. And he ranks none as being up at his level.

Perhaps that is why I witnessed a rather bizarre protocol when Ram Dass (acting as go-between) brought the famous guru Muktananda to see Sai Baba. Muktananda was the one waiting in the outer court. Muktananda was the one visiting Baba. (In the end I had to be the one to take the risk, violating all protocol, of breaking into Baba's inner chamber where he was having an interview. He did for me, in those days, what he almost never does. He left the meeting and walked with me down to the large group surrounding Muktananda awaiting him. He seemed to do it in part to satisfy my desperation, which had been added to by Ram Dass' own desperation and embarrassment.) It was a cryptic meeting where the two talked to one another on a level that no one could follow—not even the oldest Indian devotees who knew all the languages.

The famous Siddha-power guru Muktananda, whose world we will investigate later, claimed to have his explosion of enlightenment in his late thirties. (Meher Baba and Yogananda, by all evidence, made the same claim in their twenties, Maharishi in his thirties, and so on.) But Sai Baba claimed to be God-conscious from his childhood, indeed from his birth. He did not need to go through the bizarre agonies of these mortal adepts. They all needed learning experiences and their own masters and gurus. Baba had no course of study and no guru. He did not spend thirty years in the wilderness like Muktananda.

The explosion of enlightenment came to Baba as a youth, if not before. Knowing the implications of this in Vedanta, when I first met Baba in Ananthapur, I was awed all the more, for I too appreciated its magnitude. I had come to India in 1969 with total abandon after graduating from the University of Virginia. Baba, if he was what he claimed to be and what Indians believed him to be, was the returned avatar of this world, of immensely higher magnitude than the semi-avatar I had previously followed,

Paramahansa Ramakrishna, the Bengali who died a hundred years ago. It had taken an infinity of experiences to bring Ramakrishna to the top so that he 'merged with God'. What all this meant to me I cannot tell. Suffice it to say I was to become the equivalent of Sai Baba's Apostle Peter, a sold-out, inner-circle disciple who had far more access to Baba and far more privilege than any of the other Westerners. The only ones as close or closer were fewer than ten Indians who had been with Baba for at least fifteen or more years. And they, like me, were the envy of the Indian world.

The beautiful Indian girl in Delhi had referred to the handful of famous gurus now captivating the West as being 'export items'. She did not believe in them, nor did a majority of Indians. But she and India did believe in Sai Baba. What was it about Baba that mesmerized the land from the Indian viewpoint?

His credentials are awesome by Indian standards. India has been awaiting such a God-man, who could be impressive enough to vindicate its spiritual path, its system of philosophy, its entire history. He would be the one to counterbalance India's impoverishment in those areas of material achievement where the West reigns supreme. He also by his very existence upholds the brahminical caste system—a system that is the life-blood of India's elite Hindu rulers, and a system that is coming more and more into the spotlight of national criticism. There is a vested influential group that stands behind Sai Baba, numerous highborn magnates of the land—India's Rockefeller, Mellon, and Hearst, those who own production, and the media, and the banking system. Sai Baba vindicates India's legacy of spirituality and spiritual superiority.

Many Indians have told me, 'Even the best of the well-known gurus is a thousand-rupee note. But Baba is the thousand-petaled lotus. He is Param-Brahman, Siva-Shakti, Bhagavan.' (These are names for God.)

The question has been asked me, 'How can Baba be born in the desert wilderness of one of the poorest states in India, in obscurity, in a mud hut, in an area far removed from the twentieth century, and rise to the spotlight of the nation?'

My answer was and is,

'Something supernatural has intervened—the powers that be.'

My figure-ground perspective on the supernatural events has changed, for sure. But something did happen when the 'Explosion' took place. The chemistry of Enlightenment always fascinated me. It happened to Baba, as mentioned, when he was just a youth—unprovoked and without a guru. For now, perhaps it is best if we peer at his moment of Explosion from outside, in its historical framework as described by pundits who chronicled the event.

The setting

In the 1940s, when Baba was a youth, the Penukunda District, in which Puttaparthi lies, had no buses or cars. Travel was by bullock cart. There were no phones, no plumbing, indeed nothing to bring it into the twentieth century. It lay, timelessly, in the wilderness.

The night of my first bus ride to Puttaparthi, Baba's main abode, I observed that it had taken over ten hours to go a hundred miles. Each ten miles farther into Andhra Pradesh convinced me (and this was in 1969) that things could not possibly get any more primitive. But they did. The landscape went from desolate to more desolate, knotting and twisting in the moon- and starlight into all sorts of weird shapes like giant cryptic writing, which seemed to suggest a supernatural numinous quality within the terrain itself. By this point the road was more of a giant water-buffalo path, crossing rockbeds and streams, dropping sharply and climbing at hideous angles.

I reckoned then that it was,

'. . . more reminiscent of the bygone eras of the *Ramayana* than the twentieth century. The final hub of our journey abolished the last traces of civilization as we entered the incredible silence of the night air and the absolute piercing brilliance of the stars above us. Not so much as a cloud could be seen in the arid sky above us to obscure so much as a photon of starlight, lifting us at times, so that we seemed to be veritably perched on the shores of space.'

If you were to summon ancient India of millennia past in a time machine, this is what it would be like.

This never-changing terrain, sitting beyond time, was what I used to refer to as a 'perfect greenhouse for an avatar'. A suburb in twentieth-century Chicago would have been a devastating experience for the young Baba to grow up in. Some opportunist would doubtless have appeared and seen a business opportunity and taken the young Sai Baba on the entertainment circuit, if providence had landed him in America. But out here it was perfect. This remote, pristine world was inhabited by peasants and simple folk who were in a perfect mind-set to accept a human God. Peopled with men and women who consecrated everything to their gods, to whom the occult—from astrologers, to black magicians—was an everyday phenomenon, this area of Andhra Pradesh practiced and believed in the supernatural. The stage-door of village-India stood wide open for its millennial drama to begin once again, but with Kalki this time instead of Krishna as the star performer.

Even the name of the village Baba was born in contains meaning based on some distant event: Puttaparthi. 'Putta' is the native word for 'an ant hill in which a snake lives', and 'Parthi' means 'multiplier'. It means 'ant-hill city in which snakes live in the ant hills', based on an ancient legend of a cobra cursing the local cowherds. Hence the religion, the natives say, has been accursed and its once abundant farming has been dried out. The area is also fairly well-endowed with cobras. As the symbol of Shiva, they have been honored. Snake shrines can be found at the base of trees and in the hills. The region is well-known for sorcery and the black arts.

Baba's moment of birth on 23 November 1926, Hindu astrologers say, was during a conjunction of supreme importance. It was that same year that Sri Aurobindo, the renowned Indian sage and yogi, announced his vision of light crashing down from the stellar regions to the earth in the region Baba was born. And signs followed this advent.

Stringed instruments would twang around the house at night, near Baba's crib. Then a cobra was found lying in bed beside the infant Baba. This was the sign of Shiva. The infant was given multiple consecrations to the gods, especially to Shiva. He was not of the Brahmin caste, but he was still referred to as a Brahmin child. For a period of time he refused food from his family as Brahmins do if it is not cooked by a Brahmin. He told them he was being fed by an 'Old Man'. Some felt this enigmatic figure

19

was the reappearance of the Old Shirdi Sai Baba.

At eight Baba was manifesting signs. (I have called him Baba for convenience; his name was still Sathyanarayana Raju.) His schoolmates gathered around him. Out of an empty paper bag he pulled out varieties of sweets not available in the area. When asked about it he said that a certain 'Grama Sakti', or powerful spirit being, obeyed his will and gave him whatever he wanted. Then one ominous day a teacher encountered Baba's invisible agency. He had unfairly punished Baba by having him stand up on a table. When the class ended and it came time for the teacher to get up from his chair, he could not move. He was held down by some massive force. A psychic whammy. And when he did manage to get up, the chair stuck to him. He battled helplessly. The moment he released Baba from punishment, he was freed. Awe spread through the neighborhood. Meanwhile Baba's reputation for materializing items not found anywhere in the region increased. Baba was already semi-divine.

Then Baba became interested in acting. The village troupe of players, according to custom, would have plays about the gods and legends. This has always been a mainstay religious diet of rural India. One night one of the gods seemed to manifest through the young Baba. The troupe became alarmed at what they had to deal with. Narasimha Deva, the man-lion avatar, 'took Baba over' and it needed a roomful of men to hold him down. He was finally pacified by a traditional act of worship given that particular Hindu god. Baba later joined the troop and became a versatile actor, adept at playing roles of either sex (as happens with many Indian boys as it is usually the males who act).

Explosion

Then the big transformation took place—the child hit the power line when he was thirteen. The cosmic personality took over with such force that his family did not recognize the former child, and it worried them. Events are a little garbled by now but the outline goes like this.

On 8 March 1940 at seven in the evening, perhaps on a hillside, Baba suddenly screamed violently and collapsed. His body became stiff, his breathing faint and he seemed unconscious. No one really knows what happened. He remained unconscious through the night. People were worried. They suspected that the local evil spirit in the cave known as Muthyalamma, had taken possession of him.

Volunteers hurried to the cave and offered sacrifices to the demon spirit, laying flowers before its shrine while breaking a coconut. Immediately the unconscious boy muttered, 'The coconut has broken into three pieces.' When the volunteers returned, they reported this was so.

Doctors called into the area had no idea what was going on. Baba revived after several days of unconsciousness. His family was shocked. They could not recognize the new resident living within the body, for there was a complete transformation of personality. Since this incident took place at Uravakonda, his relatives wrote to tell his parents, now en route from nearby Puttaparthi.

The boy spent most of his time in silence, not answering people. Sometimes he would burst into song, poetry, long sanskrit verses, or religious teaching. Wisdom came from out of nowhere. When his parents got to him, they were terrified by what they saw. His body would become stiff intermittently, and he appeared to leave his body. Baba also began to share clairvoyant perceptions of surrounding events. A neighbor was brought in and humiliated by the omniscient boy.

The district medical officer from Ananthapur was dumbfounded. Astrologers said a ghost possessed the boy. Finally Baba's brother brought an exorcist to the house. The young Baba told him,

'Come on, you have been worshipping me every day, and now that you have come here, your only business is to worship me and clear out.'

The man left in a hurry.

When the parents took the boy back to Puttaparthi, they watched his behavior with increasing fear. He would say to his sister,

'Here, wave the sacred lamp; the gods are passing across the sky.'

Often they would see violent shifts in mood. Villagers theorized he was under the powers of sorcery. Again, attempts were made

21

to get an exorcist. They took Baba to a local expert in devil-craft in nearby Brahmanapalli. The events that followed resembled medieval torture, as Baba's head was shaved, an 'x' marked on his forehead, and various similar rituals took place. The boy did not react. Pain did not seem to bother him. Finally the parents sneaked the boy away from the exorcist when they could no longer endure watching the different tortures.

Back at home, his bizarre behavior remained unchanged. Sometimes he evinced the strength of ten men, and at other times villagers reported he was 'as weak as a lotus stalk'. He argued with adults and exposed their inner secrets.

Then finally this transition period reached completion. The aberrations ended, and a new power became fully operative in the boy.

On 23 May 1940, a full three months after Baba first fell unconscious, he called the members of his family together and made his formal announcement. But first he completely disarmed them. Out of thin air he presented them with sugar candy and then flowers. The neighbors rushed in. Baba then materialized rice balls and other objects for them. The boy seemed to manifest a kind of love. His brother arrived and was so distraught he took a stick and was going to beat whatever was in Baba.

'Are you a god, a demon-spirit, or a madman?' his brother asked.

Then the announcement came.

'I am Sai Baba. I belong to the Apastamba Sutra, the school of Sage Apastamba and am of the spiritual lineage of Bharadwaja. I am Sai Baba.'

Strictly speaking, this would negate his claim of being an avatar. He claimed to be a reincarnation of one of India's most powerful godmen, Sai Baba of Shirdi. Soon they were forced to take the boy to a Shirdi Sai Baba devotee in a neighboring village. The man was skeptical. Baba materialized handfuls of *vibhuti* ash and threw the powder in all directions. The man became stunned and reverent. He felt that Sai Baba of Shirdi was speaking through the boy and asked,

'What are we to do with you?'

The answer resounded, 'Worship me. Every Thursday. Keep

your minds and houses emptied for me.'

Later, on a Thursday, someone challenged the boy for supernatural proof.

'Place in my hands those jasmine flowers,' Baba told the group.

They did. He threw them in the air and they hit the ground spelling out in Telugu the name, SAI BABA.

2

TURNING THE EARTH INTO THE SKY

Sai Baba's road to godhood burst forth from his supportive community, like a spark lighting a fire. The conflagration of notoriety spread, as word of the powers of this god-possessed boy exploded from the local level to the state level and on.

Baba quit school before he was fourteen. An early devotee built him a hall of prayer where he would reside and receive visitors. His devotees multiplied. And so did his powers. Few anticipated that one day this divine boy would grow up to be worshipped by succeeding presidents of India while his real estate spread across much of the land. Governors and ambassadors would continually cut a trail out to what is today, in that same village, Baba's main headquarters.

This headquarters is now a legal township, Baba's ashram. It is walled-in and full of housing blocks, suites, hospitals, post office, police depot, bank, cafeterias, bookstores and so on. That early one-room temple was soon abandoned for Baba to reside in a massive prayer hall, with his own private apartment connected to its upper story. Pilgrims in the many hundreds of thousands would come out to Puttaparthi annually, adding up to many millions across the years.

There are so many accounts of the miraculous it would fill a book. How many tales were exaggerated, elaborated, falsified is hard to tell. Old Andhra newspapers were full of accounts, and there were all sorts of old-timers on hand to report a range of incidents. The village has strong blocks of pro and anti people regarding Baba. But the anti-Babaites are vastly outnumbered. Streams of new faces have been flooding into that town for years. But there are locals who still say that Baba got his powers through an ancient ceremony on a mountainside where an

24

ancient, specially energized Shiva symbol is hidden. They say the powerful spirit entered the boy there, from out of the Shiva lingam (a stone penis).

I became a collector of these miraculous accounts of the young 'Bala Sai', or boy Sai Baba. If a fraction of them were true, I decided, then truly Baba was on a par with Krishna or Ram or, as Baba claimed, the returned Christ. Clearly there was always a sense of mystery, an unspoken riddle operating. That Baba manifested great personal force was undeniable. That he oozed forth a kind of sweet love, an almost sensual, honey-flavored force, I can testify. That Baba has a way of entering the minds and lives of thousands I can also testify. And what of those things he has done which we would call bizarre? They are explained as divine madness, that sacred category that Hindus use to explain such things. God-men can be a law unto themselves as history bears out in India.

For Baba would perplex people. In the early days more than now, he would fall rigid and lie paralyzed and unconscious for days. He would 'leave his body'. He would convulse. And once yearly he still insists on a particular ritual: he claims to grow in his stomach stone Shiva lingams (remember the Shiva stone on the hill?) and then he regurgitates them publicly—large egg-sized rocks. The same type of stone eggs *Indiana Jones* went after in the Temple of Doom. Some years they are emerald, others moonstone, lapis lazuli, topaz, bloodstone, and the like.

Baba would assume illnesses, refusing help, then heal himself. He would 'take on' strokes and heart attacks. One of these episodes lasted six days.

N. Kasturi, one of his inner circle, described one such occurrence,

'The face twitched and muscles drew the mouth to the left . . . the tongue lolled. The left eye appeared to have lost its sight.'

Days later Baba talked only in thick lisps. Divine meanings were ascribed to everything Baba did. At the very least he was considered to be burning away evil karma, whether locally or on a larger scale.

Tales of Baba's miracles were a staple diet which Baba's devotees feasted upon, often obsessively. Here are some of the classic ones.

25

Baba used to 'pick' fruit from a tree up a steep granite incline hundreds of feet up a local hill. He picked any sort of fruit in succession—mangoes, lemons, apples, cherries, even grapes, papaya, and thrust them into the arms of the waiting throng. One day he stood beside them on the ground. Then Baba told them to close their eyes and open them again. In seconds he appeared high above them on the ledge. He then said, 'Look at me.' At that point his head opened up and a brilliant light almost blinded them from where his head had been.

'This is my true Jyotir Swaroopa, divine form of light.'

Then there is the account of the effect Baba had upon India's preeminent nuclear physicist, Dr Bhagavantam, who has been considered numerous times for the Nobel Prize. On the sands of the Chitravati river Baba told Dr Bhagavantam, a renowned skeptic, to open his hands as he kept pouring sand into them. The doctor was explaining how energy locked up into sub-atomic particles is the smallest final quantum. Baba said no, beyond that is energy which is pure consciousness from God. At that point he stunned the skeptical physicist by illustrating how this can work. The next batch of sand poured into the eminent physicist's hand, according to Dr Bhagavantam, turned into a copy of the *Bhagavad Gita*.

Bhagavantam became a convert for life, and presently serves Baba in any way he can, usually as translator. (He was the one whom I asked to see my father in London on my behalf. Try as he might, even he did not convince my father of Baba's divinity. And Bhagavantam got his doctorate under Lord Rutherford at the Cavendish labs of Cambridge University.)

Another miracle that endeared Baba to the doctor was when Baba materialized some kind of lance and pierced the spine of Bhagavantam's son, Ram Babu, and apparently healed him of a serious spinal affliction.

The list of Baba's miracles of intervention is unending: people crying Baba's name on a crashing Indian train and having Baba materialize in their presence and save them, Baba visiting them in visions, miracles of materialization happening on countless family shrines. Baba 'appearing' in the nick of time to deliver a child about to be born to one of his women 'bhaktas' (devotees) lying somewhere on her own and in travail. These accounts read like the epics of Krishna. On and on they go. Devotees can always count on miracles at the four or five massive festivals that occur each year in Puttaparthi.

To appreciate Baba's ashram festivals, it is important once again to review the scope of the ashram-township. The township belonging to Baba extends hundreds of acres. It has apartment buildings, dorms, luxury rooms for the affluent, and the thousands of poor can still spread out their bed-rolls on the ground or on the floor of one of the big auditoriums. Many pilgrims move there to become residents of the ashram after they have built or bought a room. Most of the Bombay industrial elite have their own suites somewhere on Baba's compound. And there is always a contingent of foreigners from overseas. Most of them wish to become permanent residents, but few do. The austere hardships of the region get to them sooner or later and almost none of them can get a resident's permit unless they are from the British Commonwealth.

For me to get a resident's permit was quite an accomplishment, and again pointed to my inner-circle status. Baba wrote a note personally to the regional superintendent of police, a devotee, to declare my resident status. What made it even easier is that the man had been a fan of one of my writings, which the Governor of Assam had printed up at his own expense, and which was circulating around Northern India. And of course the ace card in the pocket was that the governor of then Mysore State (now it is Karnataka) was Dharma Vira, an avid Baba fanatic who continually came to the festivities.

The festivals captured Baba in his splendor before the minions of the land, and at times it looked as though all of India was there. Surely all of India knew about these events for they filled the India-wide magazines. (Indeed the owners of some of India's biggest magazines were Baba devotees.) And the masses knew that they were witnessing the historical actions of a global avatar, events that would rank in history with the epics of Ram and Krishna. Then too, these were moments when Baba would reveal himself in a divine disclosure, unveiling his purpose in history before an awe-struck crowd.

At one of the festivals I was at, as always sitting up at the very front almost at Baba's feet, he made the following declaration which removes any ambiguity about exactly who he claims to be:

'I am the embodiment of truth. This is the first time in history that mankind has had the chance of being with me in this number. In the Dwarka age and former ages, the Rishis would meditate for years to see me, and yet your chance is much greater than theirs. The moment you come into my presence, all of your sins are forgiven. I can give you full self-realization, and take you back to the eternal, limitless God-consciousness.

'Do not try to compare my power with those petty powers of magicians. My power is divine and has no limit. I have the power to change the earth into the sky and the sky into the earth. But I don't because there is no reason to do it. If all the fourteen worlds and planes tried to join up against me, they could not make a dent in my mission. If all the twenty-eight worlds and planes were to try to join up in opposition to me, they could not do a thing. I am beyond any obstacle, and there is no force, natural or super-natural, that can stop me or my mission. Do not lose this chance; it is more important than you will ever realize. Do not forfeit the chance to be in my presence.'

We would be assured that it was only a matter of time before the crowds got so huge that the closest one could get to catch a glimpse of Baba would be from five miles away in the densest of crowds. One of his private words to a devotee would be like a diamond on a necklace to be treasured for life because by then he would cease speaking to mere individuals. All but the inner circle of devotees would only be able to glimpse Baba from a great distance or on satellite television.

With his powers, we used to think, he could gain global attention in a second. And we used to fantasize how he might do it. Maybe he would sky-write on the surface of the moon like a child writes on the sand of a beach, or he would levitate one of the Catskills Mountains above New York City, or bring all the world's electrical systems to a stop and speak telepathically to the billions, or appear on global TV. It would be a cosmic drama, this we banked on.

But if the festivals fueled people's faith in one way, it was the 'inner Baba' that did the transforming, and that wrought deep changes in the individual. Indeed, perhaps even more significant to Baba's devotees is this well-known reality of the 'Inner Baba' and the inner world from which he operates, reaching out to the hidden recesses of the soul within each individual. This is considered his most miraculous field of operations. It is the surgery of liberation cutting the *jiva* ('soul') from the massive wheel of rebirth, *samsara*, to become a *jivan-mukti*, where the 'drop fuses once again with the ocean'.

3

THE INNER BABA AND COSMIC MIND CAMPS

There are two levels of reality at work on Baba's ashram. The outer-Baba manifestation with all the pageantry and charisma—his comings and goings, appearing for Darshan, seeing people for interviews, and so on. And then there is the 'inner Baba', that inner process at work within the souls of the devotees. It is an ancient, more traditional Indian chemistry of surrender to the guru as God. As some would say, it is an inner-plane thing.

Baba will visit his countless minions in dreams and in visions. Many will begin to get an inner-Baba voice in their heads who guides them in everything, even small decisions. In fact true surrender is to be guided by this voice in a small decision. Some strictly adhere to this and some ignore it, pursuing an even higher inner spiritual Baba, as I did.

Not all on the ashram were on the same level, to be sure. There were vast differences between people—from Calcutta Brahmins to Bombay millionaires, from simple folk to pundits from Benares Hindu University, from California groovers to Australians from 'down under'. And from devotees of long standing to those newly making the discovery, now suddenly going off like Roman candles.

Some became picayune (jot-and-tittle people) in following spiritual rules. Their days were structured to the minute. They were not necessarily regarded as spiritual giants by the inner circle. Rather their outward histrionics often seemed no more than a kind of spiritual exhibitionism. Most of us of some standing could see this immediately. And some of us had a cruel way of mimicking the routines—for instance water could only be drunk a certain way, so too with cleaning the tongue, entering a shrine, and so on. Some 'spiritual' devotees had the oddest ways of backing into rooms, or approaching the latrine. The logistics of movement, to them, became imbued with the deepest of meaning. I felt that their minds had been relegated to a kind of hell. Perhaps part of the cosmic drama was that they were in fact spiritually diminishing as the inner Baba looked on with a kind of cosmic mirth. They were becoming cockroaches in the grand scheme of things.

I was never a spiritual legalist. My evolution was the fast track, according to Baba, based on my high state of adeptship, combined with 'Baba's grace' and my attunement to what he called 'pure and subtle wisdom'. Like his long-term devotee Raja Reddy, I was an 'Advaitin', a complete non-dualist, which is the highest Vedantic tradition. To me, Baba was an outward appearance of the Static Eternal, the supreme Overmind. And consecration to him was consecration to the highest Self, the inner self. And Baba and I understood that that was what he really was, the Universal Oversoul. And I, in my true identity, was the same—namely God. Baba was not his body, and nor was I my ego. That was the teaching of Vedanta, and that was Baba's teaching to me. The peasant folk were still dualists, and worshipped Baba the way they worshipped a host of gods.

The pageantry of the 'outer Baba' kept the masses appeased and appealed to all of the traditionalists. And it kept us from being bored, interrupting what could become dry spells. Three or four times a year, the ashram became the center of very big festivals, with hundreds of thousands pouring in. They would go on for days, and some would go on for a week and a half. Baba would give public lectures, and *darshans* ('divine appearances') at which he walked among them. There would be plays, singing, musical groups, from famous singers out of the Bombay film world to classical Indian groups, while Vedic scholars would appear from all over the land, along with various yogis. All to honor and worship Sai Baba as the world avatar.

Imagine how I felt when Baba called me on stage to speak to India's ruling elite, or to sing to the masses on stage with him! It was intoxicating. I felt at times like a minor celebrity, though I was careful always to 'give Baba the glory'. It was quite a scene to see one of Bombay's multi-millionaires fall prostrate on the ground, lying flat on his face, and kissing the feet of Baba. Baba

31

was the supreme leveler—except when he chose to raise some and ignore others.

Dignitaries would at times line up for blocks to see Baba. Again, a certain quiet sense of accomplishment would fill me to know I had access to Baba at any time. I could walk right up to him. Influential Indians would approach me to convey various messages to Baba in my role as an inner-ring disciple. Occasionally I would agree but usually I would tell them that Baba knew their every thought, as he knew the thoughts of millions simultaneously, and was aware of their need. Or I would tell them to await Baba's call if it was important enough, or pray to the inner Baba. I knew that I would be deluged with requests if I became too accommodating.

Guidance systems

One could examine any of a hundred diaries and see a familiar pattern: Whether it was the wife of the Governor of Goa, or Mr Kamani the great Bombay industrialist, Dr Bhagavantam, or the diary of an American psychiatrist, the pattern of connection to an inner force was there. Though this pattern was traditional, it was also New Age. It spoke of telepathic universal access. The 'higher' one got, the more complex and tortuous this inner path would become.

There could be a hierarchy of inner signals—and sometimes the only means of verification, if you were close enough, was through the 'outward Baba'. He did this with me all the time: I would be awaiting his appearance, along with thousands, outside the prayer hall. He would pass me by, smile, and repeat something he had said in a dream the night before, or append something that had become a recurrent thought. Entire diaries were filled with tales of inner guidance. There were hits and misses. Some of these dramas Baba fully disavowed, especially among some of the more 'hysterical women'. And these could create painful 'testings'.

Guidance from the inner Baba could have the complexity of those guidance variables by which NASA communicates with the space shuttle as it tracks ten thousand curves, shifts, valences, gravitic variables, along with its own complex internal monitorings, while it transfers this information across space to banks of computers. So it was at times between the mind, the inner Baba and the outward Baba. The devotee was not always in the most secure position. Moorings of all kinds were often systematically cut.

The common fear of the devotee was that the impurity of his receiving instrument would cause garbled or confusing guidance if he had become 'impure' from subtly straying from Baba's will. A complicating factor was the fact that the Avatar was in the process of destroying the ego, so could create all kinds of confusing dramas. Almost anything could be negated or justified. And the God-man could involve the devotee in a test, or a disciplining measure, or 'divine sport' (*Maha-Lila*).

We of the Western contingent had our own share of cosmic farces, embarrassments, even disillusionments. When it got to be too much, some of the Westerners would leave. Of course they were explained away as being 'not tough enough', or 'not ready', or 'not single-minded enough', or 'without sufficient devotion to Baba'. The list of explanations could be as complex as the inner guidance variables.

Surrender often required indomitable zeal and devotion to weather the storms. This same rule has applied to most ashrams, and the chronicles of the yogis report unending trials and testings at the feet of the guru, who is a law unto himself. The ancient surgery of self-annihilation remains superhumanly tough. And for Westerners without this tradition, it has been truly alien terrain. Failure in the devotee has been interpreted in the standard way as his or her own inadequacy, and seen as the ego creating spider webs of self-protection for survival. The ego— that which has caused the grand illusion of *maya*, the breaking away from the Godhead, that false sense of things-as-separate— remains the ultimate enemy to God-consciousness. The deeper reality is the oneness that the ego refuses to acknowledge.

If the blasphemy in the Genesis story of humanity's fall was the self aspiring to become God, the blasphemy in the Upanishads was the self denying its oneness with God and insisting on separate creaturehood. The mustard-seed metaphor held—*Tat Tvam Asi*—'This Thou Art'. But returning to the Source was not easy.

33

Testings

Diaries of devotees were full of 'testings' side by side with all the blessings. People would act on secret orders, divine commands, and disclosures. And more often than not, it would turn into an effective ego-bursting experience. Throw in cross-cultural differences and taboos, and you have a formidable obstacle course and minefield for Westerners.

Baba could play upon people's emotions, their minds and their hearts, with the ease and control of a concert sitarist. He was a master. He could squeeze out of one single drama countless results. His economy of movement could only be seen as divine. It was a perfect parallel to the tales of the ancient Indian God-Avatar Krishna, who would mirthfully play with the mind-states of his female adorers, his Gopikas, as though their substance was as mutable as dreams. In a sense they became toys upon which the cosmic theater-in-the-round unfolded. The Hindus call this *Maha-Lila*, or God's mirthful play.

A mass exodus from among the Western ranks took place while I and a few others were on tour with Baba—a tour that included a dramatic Baba self-healing in Goa and a big festival in Bombay, taking up two months in all. When we returned, Baba explained to me privately that those remaining from the 'old group' were off-limits. They were tainted and had fallen from grace. I adhered to his command with an emotional brutality. They were now in the outer court. Many were personally dear to me but there was no question that obedience to Baba was the preeminent consideration. They were not even welcome at Baba's main ashram. Baba was due to return there soon, and even against his orders, they wanted to go back there and greet him as he arrived in his car.

No more special treatment would be in effect for these Westerners who before had access to the private rooms of wealthy families (who were usually in absentia). So in the midst of this outer rejection a drama ensued. This group of outcasts had been getting 'messages from the higher Baba'. And according to their sources of guidance, they were the true inner circle. I could see the set-up. To greet Baba's car as it returned to the main ashram, they skipped out of the front gate and rushed a mile down the barren wilderness road, a wild and disobedient

34

move considering their probationary status.

Down the barren road they hurried, running for a stretch, swaying a bit, skipping again, and marching with flowers in their hair, lapels, and hands, just like children showing their essential playfulness. For this enviable childish spontaneity was a hallmark of true purity and innocence. It showed that their inward nature was without blemish. The fornications of the past were just passing clouds over the clear moon of the eternal *atma* ('oversoul').

In the final lap of the journey, Baba's returning car edged around that one narrowing section of road clustered by trees on either side. Meeting him head-on was a human roadblock, smiling, singing, and prancing, then jumping up and down in jubilation as the car strained to a dead stop. It was a reminder of California flower-power be-ins in Golden Gate Park. Real Family of Man stuff—a true egalitarian memento. Inches in front of the bumper the ringleader gazed through the windshield with a goofy grin plastered across his face. The gleeful girls giggled, shrieked, and pranced, adorning the car with flower petals while the human tentacle wrapped around the car. Now for Baba's forgiving delight.

The window rolled down as two black orbs radiated fury. Then came the judgment, tearing the air with the force of a sonic boom rippling out in waves of blackness. Baba hissed at them furiously,

'Pssst. Foreign cracks, get out of the way. Go away from Puttaparthi, acting like hippies, not my bhaktas. Go, get out.'

The car sped on. Exuberance turned to wrenching despair. The inner message had betrayed them, and now they stood doubled up, feeling as though something in them had been torn out like a rotten onion-skin. They slunk back into the ashram only to be berated by an infuriated Mr Kasturi, Baba's secretary in residence. But rather than be evicted, they lay back and moaned. They were ready to lie outside the fence and die rather than leave. Their state of rejection, desolation, lasted for weeks. They were quarantined out on some roof-top enclosure where they baked through the days in the fierce magnesium-white sunlight. They balanced ever on the verge of sunstroke.

But just when so many of the Westerners seemed irreparably alienated, Baba suddenly called everyone in for an interview.

Before him was a crowd of vulnerable and broken people. And any word of kindness, at this point, would endear these lost people to Baba forever. And those words came:

'Many of you coming on a long journey to India, taking many risks, going through many difficulties. For many years searching, searching for love. You did not get mother's love in American families. See, American family is divided, selfish. Each person thinking of himself, not his duty. Not good, very bad. Parents in America give many material articles but no *prema*, no love. I am speaking of human love, not divine love. Human love far less, but still important. Without human love child is like a plant without water, withers. Growing up hurting, angry, even hating parents. Indian family different. In India, there are large families, growing together many generations, all members; fathers, grandfathers, sometimes great-grandfathers, uncles, mothers, grandmothers, many relatives. Not separating from home at twenty years like in America. Members in Indian families are loyal, very dependent. The child is molded better. He is obedient and takes pride in pleasing his family. Very afraid of displeasing parents with moral sin. Moral sin selfish. If he is bad, the whole family suffers. Yes, his mistake tarnishes the family name, and all suffer with his mistake. Now all over America there is complete immorality.

'You come here for love, the mother's love you missed? I love you more than a thousand mothers. And a thousand times more than your mother.'

There was a long pause, the silence welling underneath with choked emotion.

'This is also a privilege, because this is divine love. God's love.'

Baba gave us a long searching look.

'I would give my blood for you.'

Many of the girls from the old contingent started sniffling. I just squeezed Baba's foot, and looked up with contrite gratitude as his gaze seemed to envelop me in an oozing nectar.

'Yes, I also need your love,' Baba confessed.

The meeting ended with many people in tears. Baba's mercy seemed overwhelming. The Avatar, with the sword of perfect timing, had left his victims pierced to the heart and broken by his will. With such forgiveness, who could resist his command to

36

worship him as God, as he proclaimed in the early days? And what more suitable sacrifice than a human soul should one offer upon Baba's altar? Such was the fabric of divine timing.

Baba was the sovereign orchestrator and motivator of events. His body merely a focal point, a window, with the eternal nature residing in everything and behind everything. Baba in human form would give the teachings, the feedback, urging and goading his devotees, but the cosmic nature was seen as unsearchably vast, true Godhead. That was the force, the puppeteer, raising and dropping his devotees. Any true Indian guru fell in this light. Baba only more so.

Our mind-sets evolved. We were being deculturized on a fast-track growth curve. And we knew this had a price tag. Because like other cosmic training camps (Muktananda's, Rajneesh's) there was a dual aspect to devotion to the guru. Our community spirit had to be shut off like a switch if it got in the way of guru-surrender. I noticed that after certain festivals there was a weeding out from among our ranks of Westerners. Just now the Westerners seemed to be going through their second phase of this process, each drifting along his own privately tailored, internally-reinforced route to higher awareness. Often strangers to one another, we pursued doggedly the complex beckonings of the strand of intuitive thread within each of us. True, some of us compared notes, had heart-to-heart talks, but our courses were sealed, each balanced on a slightly different ledge up the awesome slope of *Himavat*, the mountain of truth.

In our own cosmic training camp people went through many character changes as they endured, some of them dramatic. And there were casualties, from disillusionment to insanity. My own two-year experience was so deep and extensive, and what I discovered was so extraordinary, that I wrote a book now on the stands of India disclosing this revelation—*Avatar of Night.* (It took 400 pages to do it justice.) We will get to most of these findings later. What had at first looked like the gates of Heaven, when I first entered Baba's kingdom, had suddenly one day become the gates of Hell.

Suffice it to say that there is a pattern to this 'divine madness', the reality of which is far different from what people are generally told. This will make much more sense by the time we get to

37

the second section, on the inner perspective. But first we need to see up close two other world-class models of Explosion— Rajneesh and Muktananda. This particular trek took me ten years. It was that long before I got all the data in, starting from my moment of final realization twelve years ago.

4
MUKTANANDA
HITTING THE POWER LINE

The massive, ascetic Nityananda looked like an ageing TV wrestler, with almost inhumanly severe eyes. The moment of power-transfer had come. It took place in Ganeshpur, a wilderness village in the fiery state of Maharashtra in a locale not too far from Bombay. It was the summer of 1947, when much of India still hung between the twentieth century and the ancient past. His adept, Muktananda, was about to make a timeless journey, the journey of the power yogi (the *Siddha*), but it required the catalytic power of the master guru, Nityananda or Gurudev, who was God to Muktananda and therefore worthy of worship as the supreme deity.

This voyage of consciousness, prized by the ancients, would split Muktananda into fragments, driving him to the limits of human consciousness. Unless superhumanly motivated, the normal person would give up at the first moment, so vast and haunting would be the terrors of the alien terrain. Perhaps the prize had something to do with this. That infinite desperation of the yogi. The momentum of will sufficient to pay any price to go the distance. By innuendo and teaching he had been prepared for cosmic insanity. Or perhaps even hell.

Then the subtle transfer of power came. Muktananda would describe the moment:

'Gurudev, his body close to mine, stood opposite. I opened my eyes and saw Gurudev gazing directly at me, his eyes merging with mine, in the *shambhavi mudra* (a classic posture). My body became numb. I could not shut my eyes; I no longer had the power to open or close them.

'I watched him very attentively. A ray of light was coming from his pupils and going right inside me. Its touch was searing, red-hot, and its brilliance dazzled my eyes like a high-powered bulb. As this ray flowed from Bhagavan Nityananda's eyes into my own, the very hair on my body rose in wonder, awe, ecstasy and fear. I went on repeating his mantra GURU OM while watching the colors of this ray. I stood there stunned, watching the brilliant rays passing into me. My body was completely motionless.'[1]

Then the guru made one of his characteristic enigmatic sounds, a guttural 'Hunh . . . hunh!', and bid the then prostrate Muktananda to leave his presence. A few days later the master finished the sentence with another enigmatic 'Hunh . . . hunh', a severe shake of the head, and the order '*go*'. This unleashing of energy began in Suki, a remote village in the same region.[2] And the process of transformation was virtually immediate. Muktananda would hold on to his unquestioning faith in the guru like rigging as a hurricane blew through his soul and insanity seemed a hairsbreadth away.

Muktananda was tapping into the power line. It was a revelation to his untutored mind. The setting was important: a wilderness of fields and nearby jungle, the village out of sight. He had a small *kutir*, a hut-temple where he lived alone. The villagers revered and supported him. And with the social system of India, they would obey him implicitly and tolerate almost any behavior no matter how bizarre, for such were the signs of one who was touched with divinity.

And with cosmic timing, the right 'divine personage' would appear, to guide him with the right subtle teaching needed to steer him through one predicament after another. A holy oddity would come, full of pre-omniscience regarding the turmoil within Muktananda. It was all a vast play on a huge stage, and these gurus were characters who transcended the play, privy to all the scripts. True, a word of guidance at times came none too early. Consider:

'I asked the old woman to leave and went inside my hut. I was assailed by all sorts of perverse and defiling emotions. My body started to move, and went on like this in a confused sort of way.

'After a time my breathing changed, becoming disturbed. Sometimes my abdomen would swell with air, after which I would exhale it with great force. I became frightened. My thoughts became confused, meaningless. My limbs and body got hotter and hotter. My head felt heavy, and every pore in me began to ache. When I breathed out, my breath stopped outside. When I breathed in, it stopped inside. This was terribly painful, and I lost my courage. Something told me that I would die any moment. I could not understand what was happening, who was making it happen. I felt drawn towards the mango trees. As I looked in that direction, I saw Gurudev (a vision of Nityananda) sitting between them his face toward me.

'Someone had seated himself in my eyes and was making me see things. Again I looked at the mango trees. I could see Gurudev Nityananda there. Then he suddenly disappeared. It seemed that I was being controlled by some power which made me do all sorts of things. I no longer had a will of my own. My madness was growing all the time. My intellect was completely instable.'

Muktananda entered his hut later at night.

'My fear increased every second. I heard hordes of people screaming frightfully, as if it were the end of the world. I looked and saw the sugar-cane field on fire through the window. Then I saw strange creatures from six to fifty feet tall, neither demons nor demigods, but human in form, dancing naked, their mouths gaping open. Their screech was horrible and apocalyptic. I was completely conscious but was watching my madness, which appeared to be real. Then I remembered death.'

He sits in the yogic lotus posture.

'All around me I saw flames spreading. The whole universe was on fire. A burning ocean had burst open and swallowed up the whole earth. An army of ghosts and demons surrounded me. All the while I was locked in my lotus posture, my eyes closed, my chin pressed down against my throat so that no air could escape. Then I felt a searing pain in the knot of nerves in the lower *chakra* (power center) at the base of the spine. My eyes opened. I wanted to run away, but my legs were locked in the lotus posture.

'Now I saw the whole earth covered with the waters of universal destruction. The world had been destroyed and I alone was left. Only my hut had been saved. Then from over the water a moonlike sphere about four feet in diameter came floating in. It

41

stopped in front of me. This radiant white ball struck against my eyes and then passed inside me. It came from the sky and entered me! The light penetrated all through me. My tongue curled up against my palate and my eyes closed. I saw a dazzling light in my forehead and I was terrified. I was still locked in the lotus posture. Then my head was forced down and glued to the ground.'

The night went on as other processes continued. By daybreak a new phenomenon had taken hold.

'I started to make a sound like a camel, which alternated with the roaring of a tiger. I must have roared very loudly, for the people actually thought that a tiger had got into the sugar-cane field. The impulse of this *kriya* (energy possession) lasted only a brief while.'[3]

The next night his red blood cells spun like disks and glowed a deep red, coursing through his body.

Muktananda has said often in referring to this period,

'I understood nothing about the various experiences such as the vision of dissolution and the radiant light that had come to me on the first day. Only afterwards did I learn that they were all part of a process pertaining to *shaktipat* (the divine power-touch of the guru). *Shaktipat* is simply another name for the full grace of the supreme guru.'[4]

This was the awakening process of the *kundalini*—the serpent-like energy the yogis believe is curled at the base of the spine. And its rising upward can only be handled by a well-initiated adept, driving most people irretrievably mad should they even get the mildest taste of it.

'Day by day my *sadhana* (meditative rigors) developed and my meditation deepened. Sometimes I would jump and hop like a frog, and sometimes my limbs would shake violently as though shaken by a deity. And this was what was actually happening: a great deity in the form of my guru had spread all through me as Chiti, the goddess of consciousness, and was shaking me with his inner *shakti* (power). This power of the guru's grace enters the disciple's body in a subtle form and does many great things. Just as a tiny spark falls into grass and in no time becomes a blazing fire, so the power enters the *siddha* student and, uniting with his innate *shakti*, performs many functions.'[5]

42

Days sped by as experiences flooded through Muktananda. It took a lot to become God, and the young adept knew it. His model and his goal remained ever steady in his vision in the form of the one who had already attained it—his Guru God, Nityananda. Visions of the guru appeared at turning-points to guide the young Muktananda. Between the power release, the *shakti-pat*, when Muktananda was first charged by the powerful gaze of Nityananda and then sent out by him, and the final Explosion into Godhood, nine years had passed.

Hindu gods possessed Muktananda, and materialized before him. They took him to different worlds. When the visions got to be too much, either a god or a sage would appear to interpret them. These were crucial to keep Muktananda on the path and to prevent him from losing heart, as he came so near to doing numerous times. Even with his titanic spiritual drive he needed this buffer. But even the buffer violated standard appearances and patterns. Consider one such buffer:

'A Siddha has enormous power. I used to visit Zippruana and always found him naked. Dozens of dogs and pigs would be around him while he sat peacefully in their midst. In India it is a tradition to bring a gift to a saint and not go empty-handed. Whatever Zippruana received, he would throw to the dogs and pigs who ate it. Sometimes when I came to visit him, he would grab my wallet, pull all my money out, and throw it to the animals. Sometimes there would be as much as one hundred dollars.

' "What makes you think that dogs and pigs eat money?" I asked.

'He snapped back, "Is it proper for a man to eat what even dogs don't eat?"

'That was the kind of being he was. He reclined on a pile of filth; yet he had great power, for that was his destiny. Bhartruhari, the great poet-saint, sings, "It is impossible to say a word about the ways of perfected beings or to know anything at all about their karma. Some live completely naked, lying on the earth without even a torn piece of mattress, and some live in splendor which outshines even that of kings. Some are serene and calm; others are mute all the time; still others never stop swearing and lie around like snakes." '

Even Nityananda fitted this latter category.

'If my guru Baba Nityananda happened to lie down on one side, he would stay that way for three or four hours before turning over. A sage has said that some Siddhas (power yogis) act like Siddhas while others act like madmen and still others act like evil spirits. In spite of this they are kings and not beggars.'

At times Nityananda's temper was so violent that he was unapproachable. Often he would hurl rocks at devotees approaching him the wrong way or at the wrong time. Numerous times, Muktananda had to dodge stones. Yet he considered these passing missiles blessings in disguise.[6]

Muktananda's chronicle of experiences continued:

'For two consecutive days I saw a number of different lights along with the red light. I was fully conscious of everything that was happening in meditation, and I was also happy. As I watched the lights I would see naked men and children, cows, and herds of splendid war horses. Sometimes I would see the images of the deities in the temples in neighboring villages. I would see something was going to happen, and it would actually happen. I would get a premonition of someone arriving and he would actually appear.'[7]

In his meditative visions, Muktananda kept visiting a plane he called Tandraloka, a realm spoken of in the Hindu scriptures. But all the while violent physical paroxysms, *kriyas*, attended these states. These *kriyas* were common in siddha yoga and continued to show the inward flow of energy at work within Muktananda.

Referring to these *kriyas*. Muktananda described different movements of this inward power.

'Sometimes my body would writhe and twist like a snake's while a hissing sound would come from inside me. Sometimes my neck moved so violently that it made loud cracking sounds, and I became frightened. Was it because of wind imbalance? I had many astonishing movements like this. Sometimes my neck would roll my head around so vigorously that it would bend right below my shoulders so that I could see my back. But because I did not understand these *kriyas*. I was always worried and afraid. Later, however, I learned that this was a Hatha Yogic process effected by the Goddess Kundalini in order for Her to move up through the spinal column into the *sahasrara* (the seventh *chakra* or energy center at the top of the head where, in yogic physiology, enlightenment takes place).'[8]

Animal *kriyas* would violently shake Muktananda's body.

'My identification with a lion had become stronger still. I roared so much that the cows nearby broke their ropes and ran helter-skelter, dogs barked madly, and people rushed to my hut. Sometimes I would zigzag along the ground like a snake, sometimes hop like a frog, sometimes roar like a tiger. My mind was held spellbound watching the extraordinary inner moods of the Goddess Chiti.'[9]

Again, at times Muktananda would leave his hut to wander and search for answers. After this phase he ran into Zippruana.

'He was a great Siddha. He used to go naked and spent his time meandering through the lanes of Nasirabad village. He was revered by everyone as a great being . . . He used to live where there were no people, in dilapidated houses and huts away from the villagers. He had attained a very high state of yoga. He was farsighted, which is to say that he knew about past and future events. His body had been burned so pure by the fire of yoga that no filth would touch him . . . The first time I visited him, he was defecating in a corner; as I approached, he began to rub his excrement all over his body. I sat down quite close to him and found that he emitted a sweet fragrance—he didn't smell bad at all. The next time I went to see him he was sitting on a rubbish dump.'

Muktananda inquired why he sat on a heap of filth.

'Muktananda, the filth that is inside is far worse than this. Think about it. Man's body is just a bag of shit and piss. Isn't it?'

Muktananda fell silent and remarked,

'Zippruana was a great Avadhuta, the crown jewel among saints.'[10]

One time that he saw Zippruana. Muktananda desperately needed an answer to what was happening to him in the hut with all these violent bodily spasms, the *kriyas*. The dung-covered Siddha gave Muktananda the encouragement he needed.

'This is the blessing, the initiation, the grace or *shakti-pat* of a great saint. When you receive such a great blessing, these processes occur. It is normal to see a great conflagration, ghosts, demons, yakshas, cobras, kinnaras, and all the phantoms of Shiva's army, and this has happened to you.'[11]

After this and a long discourse on the Goddess Chiti's *shakti*, Muktananda was alleviated. Muktananda declares,

'When I heard this great wisdom from Lord Zipru, I fell at his feet. How wise, how true they were. What an insight into reality he had given me. I cried, embracing him. He sat me down on his lap, licked my head, and passed his hand over it, saying, "Your glory will reach the heavens." '[12]

Muktananda was transported to blissful realms, including, he believed, a realm intersecting the moon. But his tests were not over. No sooner had he been blessed by some god in a chariot, or seen some realm of splendor, than back he was thrust again to a cosmic sewage conduit. He trudged through a dismal world of pure excreta, sinking into mounds of it, and meeting Yava, the Hindu god of death. He had been meditating on the black light.

Then the grand awakenings came. The first vision of the blue pearl. It was cosmic overload:

'I have already described the sphere of unmanifest light found in the *sahasrara* (the lotus-power chakra-center at the top of the head). One day it opened up and its light was released, and the brilliance of not one or two thousand, but millions of suns blazed all around. The light was so fierce that I could not stand it, and my courage broke down. I no longer had the power to stop my meditation. I could not get up from where I was sitting. My posture was not under my control, nor could I open or shut my eyes at will. That brilliance had drawn me toward itself, and as I gazed at it, I lost consciousness. When I recovered myself a little, I began to cry, "O Goddess, O Sadgurunath, save me," because I was afraid of dying. My *prana* (life-force energy) had stopped moving; my mind was not working and I felt my life force passing out of my body. "O Lord, O Perfect Guru," I cried, "Om, Om," and then I lost all control of my body. Just as a dying man opens his mouth, spreads his arms, and makes a strange sound, so I fell down making this sort of noise. As I fell, I urinated involuntarily.'[13]

Muktananda was getting near the really immense power lines of Explosion-point, where he as an individual would be obliterated. He would be beyond the point of no return. Superconscious states would take control of him, and his consciousness would be kicked out to more and more remote levels.

5

EXPLOSION

Then it happened—Explosion.

'The time had come for my Gurudev's command to be fulfilled. I was to reach the summit of man's fortune, which is divine realization. Once the vehicle of a spiritual traveller's *sadhana* (spiritual course) has reached this point, it stops there forever. There you may see nothing and hear nothing, but at the same time all is seen and heard, for inside you is the spontaneous conviction that you have attained everything. When an aspirant has reached there, he sits in bliss, sleeps in bliss, walks in bliss, comes and goes in bliss. From inside comes the voice, "I am that which is dear to all, the Self of all, I Am, I Am." Now once again I saw Neeleshvara, the Blue Lord, whose nature is being-consciousness-bliss.

'From within, Bhagavan Nityananda (God-embodied-as-Nityananda) seemed to shake me, and then the rays of the red aura lit up the 72,000 *nadis* (subtle nerve bundles) and all the particles of blood. Immediately afterward, the white flame stood before me, followed by her support, the black light, and finally my beloved Blue Pearl, the great ground of all. With the Blue Pearl on my meditative horizon, my meditation immediately became more intense. As I gazed at the tiny blue pearl, I saw it expand, spreading its radiance in all directions so that the whole sky and earth were illuminated by it. It was now no longer a pearl but had become shining, blazing, infinite Light: the Light which the writers of the scriptures and those who have realized the Truth have called the divine Light of Chiti (consciousness). The Light pervades everywhere in the form of the universe. I saw the earth being born and expanding from the Light of Consciousness, just as one can see smoke rising from a fire.

'I could actually see the world within this conscious Light, and the Light within the world, like threads in a piece of cloth, and cloth in threads. Just as a seed becomes a tree, with branches, leaves, flowers, and fruit, so within Her own being the Goddess Chiti becomes animals, birds, germs, insects, gods, demons, men, and women. I could see this radiance of consciousness, resplendent and utterly beautiful, silently pulsing supreme ecstasy within me, outside me, above me, below me.

'And then in the midst of the spreading blue rays, I saw Sri Gurudev, his hand raised in blessing. I saw my adored, my deity, Sri Nityananda. I looked again, and instead, Lord Para-Shiva with his trident was standing there. As I watched, He changed as Nityananda had changed. And now I could see myself, Muktananda, as I had seen him once before when I had had the vision of my own form. He too was within the Blue Light of Consciousness; his body, shawl, his rosary of rudraksha beads, were all of the same blue . . .

'Nityananda was standing in the midst of the shimmering radiance of pure Consciousness and then, as ice melts into water, as camphor evaporates into air, he merged into it. There was now just a mass of shining radiant light with no name and form. Then all the rays bursting forth from the Blue Light contracted and returned to the Blue Pearl. The Blue Pearl was once again the size of a tiny lentil seed. The Pearl went to the place it had come, merging into the Sahasrara Chakra at the crown of my head.'[14]

Muktananda lost his consciousness, memory, distinctions of inner and outer, and the awareness of himself.

In place of the former person was the walking void, the Unself, the hollow shell filled with the soul of the universe—according to Siddha Guru Muktananda. From that moment his mission exploded out into the world. Final verification came when the body returned to hollow-shell Siddha Master Nityananda. Now the outer-guru was to endorse what the inner-guru had proclaimed. The words of proclamation resounded across much of Maharashtra, and later India.

'You are no longer Muktananda, you are parambramha, you are SadaSiva . . . the great Lord Shiva, the Lord of the Universe.'

When the body of Nityananda fell away from this world, the scepter of Siddhahood went to his pupil, Muktananda.

6

RIDING THE COSMIC CIRCUIT

The explosion of light in the wilds of Maharashtra, emanating from the Blue Pearl, but from which the tiny spark originated from Nityananda in that moment of mystical fusion of eyes, required an immense journey. It came close to a miracle. From a plain-looking Indian villager wearing almost nothing and existing in Third-World poverty, Muktananda arose out of the ashes of Shiva, a quarter of a century ago. He became Muktananda the guru, a Rider of the Cosmic Circuit. From utter anonymity to world-class fame. The West, in its own existential vacuum, vacuumed up the experience of the Blue Pearl with a desperation bordering on madness. Or perhaps the spiritual explosion carried a quiet power of its own—as some say, a kind of ancient magic. For the very Unself that emerged from that hut would go from rags to Mercedes Benz limousines and chartered 747 jets.

In 1976 Muktananda Siddha Guru gained a full page in *Time Magazine International*. In the Who's Who of world figures that represents having arrived. This was a newsworthiness of the greats. *Time* gives a gleaning of what the Muktananda entourage had become:

' "In this country they have Father's Day and Mother's Day, and they might as well have Guru's Day," said the small, closely-cropped Indian dressed in a red wool ski hat, red silk robes and red knee socks. He was himself a notable guru, Muktananda Paramahansa. So, last week (August 20, 1976) at a secluded retreat that was once a Catskill Mountains resort hotel in upstate New York, more than 2,000 followers staged a day-long celebration in honor of the man they consider a saint.

'There were prayer sessions from which rose chants of Sanskrit verses. Then the blue lights of the meditation hall dimmed, and the faithful swayed rhythmically to and fro.

'Muktananda, 68, known to his followers as Baba (father), is

America's newest fashionable guru. With 62 centers in North America besides the Catskills ashram, he has attracted more than 20,000 devotees since his arrival in 1970. He has also received respectful visits from such celebrities as California Governor Jerry Brown, singers James Taylor and Carly Simon, anthropologist Carlos Castaneda and astronaut Edgar Mitchell. At home in India, too, he has a considerable following. There are centers of his disciples all over the subcontinent. He will return there this fall in a chartered Air India 747, together with 400 American devotees and a pet bull terrier. But this is undoubtedly not his last sojourn in the U.S.'

The *Time* article went on to describe the chain-reaction of Muktananda's influence and the inroads he has made into the ranks of well-educated and successful professionals. It all started with his first American and international road trip with Ram Dass. He was virtually unknown when first brought into Greenwich Village—but not for long.

The *Village Voice* eulogized this New Age landmark event along with *East-West Journal*, *Yoga Journal*, and *New Age Journal*. Ram Dass, formerly professor Richard Alpert of Harvard fame who with Timothy Leary turned the United States on to LSD-25, acted as an ambassador to this Eastern invasion, accompanying Muktananda on his first circuit of America in 1970, when he went from New York to San Francisco, ending this 1970 circuit at the Cow Palace with thousands 'blissing-out'. Meanwhile Ram Dass' runaway bestseller, *Be Here Now*, was perhaps the most seductive hook in the youth consciousness of America into the coming enlightenment. Yogic paraphernalia were in. Along with incense, people had their own shrines, favorite deities, Eastern scripture, meditative mats (doe skin being the 'highest'), Indian garb, Tibetan Tankas, thigh-bone horns, mandalas, *ad infinitum*.

From America, the ecstatic tour blew across to Australia, feeding the imaginations of throngs of 'truth-hungry' Australians, who were now disillusioned materialists ready for the initiations of higher light to explode across the world. Imagine a power yogi and an ex-Harvard professor teaming up—the timing was perfect for those receptive in the West. No PR firm in the world could have planned it better. Ram Dass was ever the charismatic, articulate proponent whose zeal knew no end, as he rode the intoxicating surfboard on out to infinity . . . just ahead of the breakers.

Ram Dass, the consummate Vedantist-Romantic, switched his classroom eloquence to the masses, to reinterpret Vedanta in fresh metaphor for the West. For Ram Dass was a living auto-biography, an experiment in consciousness-expansion for the world to see. Many could recount his obliterating meeting with power yogi Neem Karrolli Baba in the mountain ranges of North India. So his endorsement was like Calvin Klein on a pair of good jeans. Added to Ram Dass' enthusiasm was a kind of brutal self-honesty that captivated his followers even more. Boundaries lost definition. Were people coming to see Ram Dass or Muktananda? Or were they there to see a great historical precedent as perhaps Muktananda might reach over and on some vast stage give Ram Dass *shakti-pat*, full voltage, to send him soaring into Godhood forever—a gala Explosion for all to see. Ram Dass, this pioneer *par excellence* who in the sixties teamed up with Timothy Leary to usher in the age of psychedelics. If he threatened the institutions of that day, the 'straight-society', he was now taking it a step farther. The psychedelic at-one-ment had been a chemical preview of what could be attained forever with Yoga. Yoga was beyond LSD.

Was Ram Dass the mystic-in-chrysalis about to emerge as the perennial butterfly of Buddahood? The audience was certainly waiting.

When this ecstatic entourage of 1970 came to my cabin in India, it hardly seemed an accident. Their world tour from East Village and the Cow Palace of San Francisco had shrunk to a paisley Volkswagen bus, decked to the hilt in Vedantic motifs, driven by Ram Dass, accompanied by some extremely high Muktananda and Neem Karrolli followers—with that certain look of compassionate all-knowing. Nuances were all around them when they emerged. And my reunion with Ram Dass became a super *déjà vu* of some former lifetime hiatus. Perhaps we had last seen one another as relatives, parting at the Kiev Railroad station. Real Tolstoy stuff. Or one of us had been eaten by a tiger while we were meditating together on the banks of the Ganges near Benares circa 1870. (By that time Baba had taken me aside one day to assure me that Ram Dass and I were brothers from the past.)

It seemed cosmic irony that Ram Dass and I would be the liaisons for the next day's meeting between our respective gurus, Muktananda and Sai Baba. Muktananda was staying in a five-star hotel in Bangalore, fifteen miles away from Baba's Mysore retreat (formerly the summer home of the King of Nepal). My cabin near Whitefield was in the center of what had been a British farm community, in the wilderness. The entourage loved it. I congratulated Ram Dass on his bestseller, which deftly explained the subtleties of the ancient path in original metaphor and apt down-home jargon. I too was writing a work to be released in Calcutta, glorifying Baba for an Indian audience—a reverse coin of Ram Dass' efforts. Yet for now we simply relished this meeting between two beings who had reached Explosion if anyone on earth had. Within an hour we would all be meeting with Baba about Muktananda's desire. Baba would graciously agree. He would then materialize a silver pendant for Ram Dass symbolizing the unity of the world religions within a circle and a five-pointed star.

But the meeting turned out to be a baffling affair of cosmic protocol that neither Ram Dass nor myself could fully untangle. At the end we were exhausted and bewildered, as each guru seemed to be toying with the other. As I described it at the time, the whole thing felt more like the Gunfight at OK Corral. Universal love, I felt, wore strange masks. (I had to break into Baba's interview room to get him to come out, as I mentioned before. This awed Ram Dass, that I should have that kind of access.)

Baba was in the mode of blissful timelessness, as I held his hand and escorted him down to the meeting room amid the 'ooohs and aahhhs' of the yogic cognoscenti who were there to 'Be Here Now', and witness the meeting of the yogic supermen. But what emerged further to confuse the Western contingent of admirers was a cross-dialogue in an alien tongue. It was even baffling for the Indian inner-circle translators, as they tried to disentangle abstruse and ancient poetry that resembled the playful stanzas of the gods to one another in some bygone time. There was a moment when the two gurus were obviously complimenting each other on disciples. Ram Dass was singled out. And Muktananda perhaps saw in me a real firebrand of Shiva. I felt like an Angus bull on display. Baba was finally given a standing invitation to grace Muktananda's ashram.

Afterwards it was time for Ram Dass, the rest of the entourage and me to drive into Bangalore to a Chinese restaurant to try and disentangle the unfolding of the New Age. We were tired, starved, and had headaches. The only positive thing we were sure of was that a disaster had been averted, and that we had probably resolved a difficult situation better than at first appeared. For instance, what if I had not retrieved Baba and Muktananda had been kept waiting an hour instead of half an hour? What if he had left feeling slighted? We were grateful. I had been hoping Ram Dass would switch over to Sai Baba. But instead the ecstatic tour went on to Delhi and then on to Ganeshpur, near Bombay. The only cross-pollination we managed to pull off was a certain interchange of disciples between Sai Baba's centers and Muktananda's retreats.

Meanwhile Muktananda and Ram Dass were gaining momentum together. And other visits to the States would bear even greater fruit, as *Time Magazine* was to mention. Operating behind all of this was a sense of mission, a secret only privy to the inner circle. A plan was in effect. To quote Ram Dass, 'Central Casting' was amazingly enterprising.

7

SIVA-SHAKTI

What the cosmic circuit needed was an Enlightened master from the East, one who was convincingly in a state of superconsciousness, teamed up with a Western adept who could bridge the gap and translate all of the concepts into colloquial, upbeat, hip, avant-garde, and semi-scientific language. The man of Eastern vintage would have to have sufficient razzle-dazzle, enough evidence of supernatural force, to validate the intuitive intimations of Western seekers. They in turn could gloat over this discovery, saying to the establishment, 'We were right; we saw through all your games, your myopia.'

This great discovery would now become a sort of higher court which would judge the traditional foundations of Western civilization and rule them invalid. Only a new mysticism within a New World Order could work to rescue a planet on the edges of oblivion. After all, it was the old traditional systems that got the world into this mess, right? Nothing to do with anything endemic to the heart of man!

In time the New Age network would emerge with its own journalists, mystics and poets, who would derive a delicious sense of revenge from beheading one sacrosanct tradition after another. New Age politics would emerge in countercultural tabloids till that generation rose up and became the establishment. Then they could infiltrate these views across establishment media. Gradualist replacement of one generation by another could alter the foundation of a civilization in a single generation, so the theorists proclaimed.

The Riders had an audience in waiting. The foundations had been elaborately laid. To misquote Voltaire, 'If there weren't a Ram Dass, it would be necessary to invent him.' In ten years, the work of an earlier incarnation of Ram Dass had done the spade work exquisitely—in the shape of psychedelics. They were ready for the next hit. Millions of them. These were the American neo-Gandhians.

What the starry-eyed idealists and revolutionaries forgot to do was look, not romantically but realistically, at what its mystical model-state, India, had become. To quote the title of V. S. Naipaul's brilliant book, India was a *Wounded Civilization*. And the actual outworking of its philosophy produced dire and terrifying consequences, such that any Westerner going there went through profound culture shock. And the new challenge was to interpret India with carefully couched, higher abstractions, ever romanticized and sympathetic.

It reminds me of Malcolm Muggeridge as a journalist in Moscow in the thirties, a dyed-in-the-wool socialist out to prove his point at any cost. As he reports in his autobiography, *Chronicles of Wasted Time*, he delighted in the sheer game of dream-weaving and the craft of pulling the wool over the naive eyes of his adherents back home. They read his grandiose accounts of Bolsheviki idealism and conquest, as he was caught in the play of journalistic elaboration for its own sake and in his cleverness thereof, until he realized that he was the one being manipulated—by the powers in Moscow. The inhumanity of the Soviet state finally became too much, and his spree ended as he felt the hollowness of his enterprise. In the role of defender of the faith, he had lost his objectivity. He had flirted with an adventurous role until the scope of reality was soberly driven home. So too with the defenders of the great Indian romantic vision, the Indian mystical state.

I was one of the worst offenders: interpreting India through the mystic eye became a kind of pilgrimage and a token of higher consciousness. Especially since there is hardly a Westerner alive who does not go into severe culture shock upon first arrival in India—profound shock over the fusion of alien terrain, smells, poverty, crowding, and different customs. The shock can last weeks. The Peace Corps attrition rate is one of the highest in the world in India. And these are people who are well prepared. Immersion in the vast subcontinent, at the first time of asking, is traumatic. So it was with a certain delight that the 'old hands' among us in South India re-interpreted 'appearances' to new-comers fresh from the West. Things that sent them into a tailspin had entered the ordinary in our realm of experience.

I had a standard lecture to the newcomers wanting to follow Baba. One must see what appears as filth through the eyes of the gods. The sublime and the beatific hid behind every little obscenity in sight—and there were many of them to be sure. Sometimes I was eloquent. And invariably after such a discourse, I would get quagmired in dung, dysentery, and dogs, which conspired to await me on the footpath home, hidden from view. A screech or a wail here or there, and by journey's end I would be in an incoherent rage, damning the very land I had lauded. Interpreting the grotesque became a matter of will. Only in retrospect, years later, would I see my dilemma as resembling the naked king in his 'new robes'. I was his Vedantic counterpart.

Ram Dass and others (Werner Erhard, Da Free John, and so on), America's window into the East, were doing the same thing. They were buffers, interpreters, delving into both worlds and predigesting the diet. What Kipling said would never happen ('Never the twain shall meet'), was happening—but it required go-betweens. Cultural re-adaptation was necessary, and some of that was like what we were doing with our journalistic license. And at times it was a considerable challenge, requiring the intellect of an ex-Harvard professor (as Ram Dass is), combined with a broad ethnic and aesthetic intuition. What was offensive or threatening had to be modified or re-explained. People had to be gently led, perhaps seduced, into the kingdom. The ends justified the means. But only people in the know were in a position to make the decisions. The plebeians, the untutored, pre-mystics, had to be given Gerbers baby food. I did it, and Ram Dass did it. We felt, as we shared together one time, like adepts pre-selected and standing in the gap. It was a heady responsibility.

Ram Dass spoke to tens of thousands in America, and virtually no one in India. I spoke to groups of the same size, but under Baba. I felt more in the role of ambassador to the Indians, getting them to put aside their differences for the coming cultural fusions. This meant removing them from traditional cultural pride and caste superiority, and using their own beliefs to do it. Ram Dass was hitting the West. In my book, *The Amazing Advent* (Calcutta), which I cancelled the day of publication (we will see why later), I was addressing India. Apart from glorifying Baba, I had to make sure Indians did not make the mistake of seeing us Westerners as second-class spiritual citizens, but as their brothers from afar, brimming with spiritual vitality and creativity. Privately I saw us as new blood injected into a decaying system.

Those in the West naive about the impenetrable pride of Brahminism have no idea what I was up against. The caste system has outlived Gandhi, and those at the top have no intention of vacating the apex of the pyramid. As Ram Dass' counterpart in India, a go-between, I had to challenge traditional Indian prejudices under the seal of Baba. And then they would listen. And they did. Such, I learned, was spiritual diplomacy. But, like secular diplomacy, it required flexibility and bending the rules. America too needed diplomacy. But even more it needed razzle-dazzle. Here was an audience jaded from Hollywood electric effects—*Star Wars* and everything else that Spielberg and Lucas could throw. The East Village needed to reek with phenomena reminiscent of *The Ghostbusters*.

When people, for the first time in the States, were hanging from the rafters in the East Village watching Ram Dass and Muktananda on the stage together, they were hungry for special effects.

Muktananda's impact was overwhelming. He was fierce with energy. People vibrated in his energy field as he threw out waves of power into the audience, thunderbolts of *shakti-pat* through gesture and powerful gazes. Ram Dass took the back seat and gave Muktananda support. Other gurus had come and gone—Guru Maharaji, Maharashi Mahesh Yogi, Yogi Bhajan, Satchidananda, Meher Baba, Krishnamurthi, Paramahansa Yogananda, and others. They reached the way back to the turn of the century when India's first 'Enlightened' ambassador of Vedanta came to the States, Ramakrishna's premier disciple, Vivekananda, who spoke at the World Parliament of Religions in Chicago and turned them on their ears. Then, there was a small circle. Now, things were going full tilt. Time was being compressed. And the old order had no idea how fast things were moving nor how deep the changes were.

The culture slept like Gulliver being roped down by Lilliputians in his sleep. Public memory lasted as long as an event, then soon evaporated. Lenin had observed in the twenties that if you can captivate the minds of a generation, it is only a matter of time until they get to power and replace the earlier generations. This was the fastest means of revolution imaginable, with almost no bloodshed. America was too busy licking its wounds from the debacle in Vietnam, and having a national orgy of self-hate. Patriotism and values were out of fashion. Again, the role of Ram Dass and others as New Age catalysts cannot be fully appreciated apart from this perspective.

So one can imagine the incredible readiness of those cramming into the big hall in the East Village. The American folk guru, Ram Dass, was finally bringing them evidence from India in one of its most powerful Siddha power yogis. They swayed and chanted so loud that they almost blew the roof off, levitating to a spiritual Himalayan kingdom on a cloud of incense while colored lights bathed the surging crowd. The air was electric with expectation. And every conceivable vestment could be seen, from Indian peasant garb to high fashion, as though representing the tribes of the earth. But the theme was Hinduism, with an eclectic undertone from other traditions. Sitar music played, meditation mats and chairs filled the stage, and pictures of deities, gurus, and symbols surrounded the auditorium. All kinds of Eastern groups were represented in the audience, paying homage to the unity among them all.

Soon ashram land would be donated to Muktananda. Then houses, hotels, would follow. And a network would be formed. Muktananda could hold retreats on his own American land where thousands could come and sit at his feet. Because that is the bottom line with the guru—you sit at his feet.

Who is the guru? Muktananda tells them a thousand times, 'The Guru is God'. You therefore sit at his feet. The guru is deserving of worship, as God on earth. He is divine. He is one with God. And the role of the disciple is very easily defined. It is absolute obeisance, absolute surrender. And here is where you need a Western lubricant to oil the works, and interpret a wholly new concept to a culture not used to this sort of thing. Autonomous youth used to anarchy and doing their own thing must be roped down to absolute surrender in a Guru Kingdom with Him as God. If in the past they rebelled and were provoked by the slightest hint of authority from their parents or schools, now they were to be prepared for the gear change of their lives—serfdom to the guru.

Those following Muktananda back to Ganeshpur would find out. When he said, 'Swab the commode at four a.m.', you did exactly that without a hint of reluctance. If a hint of disagreeableness emerged, medieval guru laws were enforced—silence, fasting, further duties, at times beatings. And if there was still non-compliance, the *sadhaka* was cast out on his ear. Simple. The rules had been the same for Muktananda under Nityananda; why should he change them for Westerners?

Westerners had a problem. When the honeymoon ended it really became evident. They had little will-power, little trust. They were soft and wanted to do their own thing. The price tag was high, and hence there was a high failure rate. And those who remained got into an ego thing at times, where their ability to stay on was now a feat equivalent to a Colorado rock-climbing contest. But at least they were caught in the net, and in the process of surrender, so that the ancient chemistry of guru-surrender was taking its effect. And when things got tough in medieval gurudom, they could hold on to memories: earlier peak experiences of LSD, things the guru had told them, psychic experiences back home, memories of cosmic-circuit figures, hero figures who had gone the distance, and the pride of their present status in the yogic Marines—a small but select group.

But they were only beginners. And they would run into things way over their heads. Even the Ghostbusters would have problems in some of these areas.

8

COSMIC TRAINING CAMPS

Two things became the main events at Muktananda's training camps, be they in New Jersey or Ganeshpur. There were Yogic fireworks, the *kundalini* energy travelling up the spine with its concomitant range of experiences, all triggered of course by the guru's touch (*shakti-pat*). And there was the crucial surrender to the guru and all that that entailed. Enlightenment was assured if this ancient path was adhered to.

Not that the teachings didn't get complex, they did. For Muktananda's Vedantic discourses could be exhaustive. Like Nityananda, he could speak to the local peasants as though they were children. Or he could switch gears, and mesmerize the most learned Brahmin pundits and shastris who were scholars in Vedanta. A guru does not rate if he does not attract a contingent amongst these ancient cognoscenti. I recall that Sai Baba could boast the largest following from this segment of Hindu society—famous Sanskrit scholars, professors from Benares Hindu University, and so on. Muktananda too had his contingent.

If Ram Dass had enticed these recruits with the nectar of teaching, Muktananda was hitting them with the lightning bolts of Shiva. In fact he was like Shiva, the destroyer in India's trinity of Gods. Muktananda was a Shivaite, a follower of Shiva. And this could mean brutally decapitating the ego with any psychic or yogic means available in a vast arsenal. Here too, Ram Dass' experiences under his former guru, Neem Karoli Baba, would be a model. One had to understand that Love could now wear any mask, and do anything. Love had been redefined.

Love could act as a destroyer. That is what Ram Dass learned in the remote village of Nainital, as he meditated for twelve hours a day in a little hut, or temple, depending upon the season. Ram Dass, on his American tours, had prepared them for hard times and alien experiences. For again, the bottom line was the death of the ego. Something in these aspirants had to be destroyed. 'Remember, the you who is the essence of you is God,' Ram Dass had told them. That means that your little down-home ethnic American identity is not you—it is your ultimate enemy masquerading as you. So what do you do with this comfortable little ego? You destroy it. With some people it happens fast, with others they hold on and dilly-dally. Ram Dass confessed to enjoying the nuances of enlightenment on the way, so was delighting in the exquisiteness of the experience, and therefore was in no rush.

Ram Dass was eclectic enough to retrieve almost any teaching to fit the scene, whatever the scene was, from his vast array of mystical knowledge. And he could shift gears skillfully. This might mean a delay in his enlightenment, but people were willing to pay that price just to watch him evolve. And so was he. People were also willing to imitate this eclectic approach, which they did. Not that this was a cop-out, it was merely a path up a mountain bearing an infinite variety of paths.

Those who bailed out of Muktananda's ashram in Ganeshpur needed interim phases of *sadhana*, or spiritual evolution. Sometimes that involved seeing an old girlfriend, or overdosing on movies or banana splits back home. But Ram Dass had covered all of this in *Be Here Now*. He confessed that at times even he had been copping out. Later, he would see some of these diversions as a form of Tantra (we will get into this later). Not all Indians would understand this 'Pop, Op' yoga. But then again, there were a lot of things they did not understand. And this would create a whole area of spiritual politics to occur between East and West in the future. Some Indians would even complain of a 'double-standard' for Westerners, as they saw Western wants being accommodated to. They would wonder, these Indian sadhakas, in their most cynical moments, whether it had anything to do with money. But again, since the guru is God, he can do anything. He is even free to change the rules.

But the big endurance contest was to get these new recruits from the West to endure the kinds of Herculean experiences of alien terrain and mind-shattering insanity that Enlightenment requires. Muktananda and Nityananda absolutely had their brains blown out. No doubt about it. 'Nobody was home,' as

Ram Dass used to say. And like a good wine-taster, he could vouch for the bouquet of the sample. Whoever Ram Dass approved of, at his level of consciousness, was approved of by all—a kind of argument by authority of higher consciousness. And Ram Dass could be eclectic about this as well. For there was a host of beings out there who were enlightened. It was like driving along and then picking up an angel hitchhiking.

As Ram Dass said to some vast auditorium in his continuum of dialogue, referring to the savor of experience,

'Kali is an aspect of the Divine Mother, but what a mother to have. She's really gruesome. She scares the hell out of most people. You know why she scares them? Because they want to hold on to who they think they are. She's the fire of purification. She's going to take every single solitary bit of their stash and what will be left are just pure souls floating up into the One.

'At first, when you have just started that journey back to God, every time you see Kali, who confronts you with all the things you're afraid of—disasters or accidents or you get mugged or you get raped or you lose your job or something 'awe-ful' happens—you say, "Oh get away from me. I want happiness. I want pleasure. I didn't know this was part of the bargain." But later on, as you become more conscious of where the journey is going, you say, "Come on baby (Kali), give it to me . . . Ah cancer, far out." '.[1]

Such wisdom could turn into cosmic humor, as it did with me in South India as different members of my group went through various trials and hardships. In fact trials were the beneficent hand of Shiva. And we had many chuckles along the path to Enlightenment, as indeed many of the masters do. Some cosmic training camps are chock to the brim with humor.

9

SPITTING LIGHTNING

When I was near Bangalore ten years ago the Western disciples of Muktananda were forming their core group. They watched others come and go. The rule was that you had to settle for your one guru once you found him. They were not enamored with the musical-chairs approach. Theirs was an olympian's mentality—you never look up from the dirt until you have either won or died trying. I could appreciate this resolve. A certain ruthlessness of will always marked the top adepts.

These inner-circle followers would lay down their lives before the powerful Siddha guru and allow the massive voltages of *kriya* energy to surge through them and purify them. Yes, there were misunderstandings and casualties from out of Ganeshpur. But there always had been. You had to pay the price of surrender with a will like a flint. 'Never cop the cold region.' It went back to braving the alien terrain. Muktananda spent decades on the path, at times inhumanly painful and frightening. They were warned all along. And it was drilled into them repeatedly that it took utter abandonment, a certain desperation of will, otherwise failure was guaranteed.

As all the great Masters, Muktananda had yet to pass on the fire of the blue pearl before his time on this earth ran out. There was no time to play around. No spiritual tourism. And these people understood this.

The voltage surging through Muktananda was no joke. It had to move on before the body dropped away. It needed—this *kundalini*—a very prepared host. What was utterly vital was the final interpretation of the supernatural event. One should not glibly discard the entire category of the supernatural because of bogus examples. It is much more complex than that. That would be too simple a way out, posturing as 'intellectual' and 'rational'. Here is that nether world between the rationalists and the

64

occultists. That would be like someone holding up a counterfeit Modigliani, boasting, 'That proves the real one does not exist'.

The frustrating thing is that paranormal investigations using the scientific approach often unearth bogus as well as genuinely inexplicable events, sometimes side by side. The history of mediums is full of 'in-trade' cons which are nothing but stage magic, from floating horns to table rapping. But then you encounter Peter Hurkos who helps the Boston police find the Boston Strangler plus scores of other killers.

And there is always that original paranormal hook that pulled in Ram Dass, catching him completely off-guard, stunned—this little man in a blanket in the Himalayas who knew things about him that not even his Freudian analyst of five years knew. This included obscure childhood details. Nor had Neem Karolli Baba any forewarning of Ram Dass' appearance in Nainital. After all, he had collided with a Neem Karolli Baba disciple, Bhagavan Dass, at the Blue Tibetan restaurant in Kathmandu, hundreds of miles from the old guru. And their arrival together was un-announced.

Some of this a good mentalist like Kreskin can duplicate, but not all of it. And an expert can see the difference. That is why Kreskin, who is one of the world's best mentalists, believes in the real thing. This is not an easy field of knowledge to deal with. It goes back to the Magi of the Pharaoh of Egypt who could use their occult powers to match Moses right up to a given point and no further. But they still did things that would impress most people, even though these ancient sorcerers were anything but saints.

Meanwhile, back in Ganeshpur, the young disciples would be up at four a.m. to meditate while the power of their master magician guru came cracking through their spines as they con-vulsed through these *kriyas*. *Kundalini*, the ancient serpent power, was at work 'purifying them' to be fit vehicles for full voltage. Until then, it would kill them. They had to unknot their nerve centers, the *chakras*, to enter the garden of the gods and allow the serpent to work up to the garden of Enlightenment. There were seven stages, seven nerve centers. The power had to work through each, from the groin to the top of the head. Then they, like their guru, would experience the blue pearl, and drink of the nectar of the gods, the nectar of immortality. They would then have solved the riddle of life.

The whole yogic science of Ayurveda and Hatha yoga went into the glandular and neurological implications of Enlightenment, when full voltage comes on and pours through the physical frame. Hence special diets, and regimens. Hence understanding, for these Western adepts, of the deepest secrets of India's mysticism and yoga as outlined in modern and ancient texts. So the disciples of Muktananda read after meditating. Then they performed yogic exercises; *pranayama* (breathing), *mantras* (chanting the divine name of Shiva or their guru), and *asanas*, or what the West calls yogic postures, the mere tip of the iceberg of Hatha yoga. And with surrender, and with preparation, and with the grace of the guru, Muktananda, one day the current would come on full voltage and there would be 'nobody home just the soul of the universe,' as I used to say when I was with Sai Baba, 'residing in an empty shell of a body'. The original resident, the original ego, will have been fully vacated.

And like us under Baba, they too had their share of Mensa types. They were not all idiots by any means. This is a pattern in many advanced groups such as this. Some of the most brilliant people become deeply attracted, and pulled into the philosophy of Enlightenment—because its range and subtlety can be astounding. And a dullard quite frankly does not have the aptitude to comprehend Advaita monistic philosophy any more than a normal IQ can cope with the range of any number of deep subjects. It is often ordinary minds that laugh off things that are complex and esoteric such as mysticism, a field that they cannot understand. So it was with a certain impatient disdain that we wrote off and caricatured those simpler minds who smirked or cracked 'down-home' grins at the mention of something they did not really understand. The grin indicated that a mediocre mind had reached boiling point and had maxed-out, like a red flag. There was, no doubt, a gap in communication between New Age seekers, mystics, Eastern adepts, and 'ordinary people'. And the contempt was sometimes hard to hide.

However, the harsh school of ego-death would in time eliminate any ego-oriented sense of superiority. For this was a ground rule. After all, 'they' are the ones who are ignorant, so be patient. Such was the invariable by-line when letters from home were opened and the gap of communication reached ever greater distances. There would even be an occasional scream of disgust—on the Muktananda ashram and on the Sai Baba ashram—when the relatives of some of these people shared their feelings and fears. Again what made this complex is that the intuitions of these relatives could have, at times, been on target (you don't need to be a genius to sense danger), but their plain display of non-comprehension of the subtleties of mysticism disqualified their opinions in the eyes of the adepts.

And at times the adepts were technically right—they knew their relatives did not see it for what it was. They were the cosmic Aborigines, looking at microchips and laser crystals and seeing sticks and stones. This is what the 'ordinary mind' did with the cryptic statements of the gurus and the Koans of the Zen masters, statements that were pregnant with multi-level meanings or that seemed to tear into human nature like the levels of an onion, exposing layer after layer. That is what Neem Karolli Baba did to Ram Dass. But Ram Dass saw the pattern, he caught the subtlety. Some of these statements had devastating penetration.

In describing the experience of Muktananda's power touch of *shakti-pat*, Karen Alboher's tale is not uncommon. Her meditations took off after that initial meeting with the guru in October 1970 at the Unitarian Church in San Francisco. Ram Dass introduced the guru, 'rhapsodizing about his high consciousness and powerful vibrations'. Many people felt the force. Karen was a model and says,

'I hadn't given much consideration to where my lifestyle was leading. After meeting Swami Muktananda, however, there was a noticeable change. My mind became so indrawn, at times, that I was forced to sit and meditate.'

Her meditations completely changed course.

'I became aware of a shaft of golden light that ran the length of my spinal column. It was this golden light that saturated my head during meditation. I also saw mystical symbols located at various centers in that column of light, and a coiled serpent at the base. These visions of Kundalini were so fascinatingly beautiful.'[1]

Guidance, according to standard lines, pursued Karen. Muktananda invited his promising pupil to India. She accepted.

67

Before leaving, she was in the middle of a difficult yogic posture, 'when I felt a strong fluttering in my heart. I thought that I was going to die (sound familiar?), but the fear soon passed, and I had the sensation of travelling at tremendous speed.' She appeared in a luscious garden and within it 'I saw the imposing figure of a lotus-seated yogi who radiated a tremendous energy.' When she arrived on Muktananda's ashram in Ganeshpur, India, she recognized the garden. And she recognized the yogi in her vision from a portrait of Nityananda, the guru of Muktananda.

Karen fell into line at Ganeshpur. She would sit in the dark meditation hall where hundreds of disciples at times lined the walls. The fireworks displays would begin. Then she could hear Muktananda leave his apartment and enter. At one point, 'He just stood there, but in a second I felt a jolt, like a flash of lightning, enter my heart, completely obliterating any self-awareness.' The guru would be standing silently before her.

That was only the beginning of the pilgrimage. Fittingly, she would start off with a real honeymoon.

'For the next three days my body was pulsating with the energy that surged through it. I laughed ecstatically, wept with happiness, felt energetic enough to hold the universe in my hand, and hungry enough to devour all the earth's food.'

Later Karen would return to the States with Muktananda after three years in India. The team was now getting prepared for his next big tour. Meanwhile, hers was an average testimony. Some however were not. Kundalini had other places to go.

10

KUNDALINI AT MIDNIGHT

Even the case-hardened wills of a portion of Muktananda's inner circle could not weather all of the tests. The bizarre they could endure, insanity they could endure, even monumental inconsistency between the guru's divine proclamations they could get by with. But the one thing that kicked apart the most dedicated blind faith of at least some of them—yes, some held tenaciously through these tests—was the nocturnal stirrings of the Kundalini. Kundalini at midnight on the rampage, as it were.

It was more than just a crackle or two up the spine. And it was more than just the disembodied presence of the master. Sometimes it was Muktananda actually moving about in the body physical, going beyond the requirements of his astral duties. Sure, if you are into cosmic farming you have to make sure all the heifers are in good shape: they should be growing. And there should be food and water. They need regular sleep. They must be able to produce rich milk, and should be good and solid. The dairy-farming analogy holds. A farmer proud of one of his stock, especially one in the blue-ribbon category, will occasionally put his arm around the cow and lean on it, stroking it, patting it, running the well-trained palm over the nose and feeling the bristles. There is an ontological gulf between the two, to be sure, but a fondness does exist. The two have an understanding.

One of the young heifers, of extremely worthy stock, who managed to escape 'special treatment', I had earlier met in India in 1970 when I was a firebrand within the Sai Baba inner circle. This pretty girl was as intensely devoted to Muktananda as I was to Sai Baba. He was thrusting her quickly to inner-circle status. When she visited us and Baba in Puttaparthi in 1970, I was amazed that she could still persevere with Muktananda after having seen Sai Baba. But 'Chandra' (her Indian name) was adamant. An old friend of hers from the guru-trail days in the

United States named Surya Dass—now in our group—was trying to woo Chandra to stay. Nothing doing. She knew who her guru was. She would have been a worthy addition to our fold, I felt. But I became impatient with her adamant position and ended up talking down to her. She tasted of the spiritual nectar of our community, oooohed and ahhhed at Baba, but then returned to Ganeshpur with her head held high.

Chandra and at least fifteen others of long standing fled Muktananda in 1980. Virtually all were interviewed by a staff writer for *The Whole Earth Catalog* quarterly journal, *CoEvolution* (Number 40, Winter, 1983). Perhaps what got the interest of William Rodarmor who wrote the article 'The Secret Life of Swami Muktananda' was an open letter by Stan Trout, who I believe was with Ram Dass when he and the Muktananda contingent visited us in Whitefield. By the time of the defection, Stan Trout, like Chandra, had been with Muktananda for over ten years. He had been the ashram director as well as a teacher. Stan's name then was Swami Abhayananda. Meanwhile Chandra rose in the ranks and became head of food services while her husband Michael Dinga was a foundation trustee (he had to co-sign for deposits in Muktananda's Swiss account) as well as head of building and construction.

What finally got to them? Those secret activities, that's what.

Chandra would be in the kitchen as the humidity of Maharashtra soared. She and the girls would be cooking for hundreds. A film of sweat would cover their bodies as they scoured the kettles, cooked and baked. Now and then the god-man would creep through the back door to taste the goodies. A swat here and a little smack there. Laboring rumps and drooping goodies slavishly straining in labor over soojie kettles and candy boards. All was well on the cosmic farm. As Chandra often saw and eventually commented,

'Whoever was in his kitchen was some way molested.'

And in good time the guru would comment to Chandra about one of her laborers,

'Sex with Nina is very good.'

The girl's mother would later be made a swami.

Chandra was able to rationalize many of these exploits until it happened with another young friend whom it traumatized

70

especially. It also came up against his famous claim to celibacy. But one day Muktananda would proclaim,

'I don't have sex for the same reason you do: because it feels so good.'

Why did he have to make this defense? Chandra's husband Michael Dinga provides the answer. Regarding the Siddha's sexual exploits, the ashram trustee commented,

'It was supposed to be Muktananda's big secret, but since many of the girls were in their early to middle teens, it was hard to keep a secret.'

But what were the logistics? The footprints of nocturnal movement were not too hard to find. The above article reports:

'Another of Muktananda's victims was a woman I'll call Jennifer. She says Muktananda raped her at the main Indian ashram at Ganeshpur in the spring of 1978. He ordered Jennifer to come to his bedroom late one night, and told her to take off her clothes. "I was in shock," she said, "but over the years I had learned you never say no to anything that he asked you to do . . ." '

The guru had something like a gynecologist's table in his room. Michael would later realize that Muktananda had built it.

The article reported,

'Muktananda had intercourse with Jennifer for an hour, she said, and was quite proud of the fact. "He kept saying, 'Sixty minutes.' He claimed he was using the real Indian positions, not the Westernized ones used in America." While he had sex, the guru felt like conversing . . . "The main thing he wanted to know was how old I was when I got my first period . . ." '

When she was trying to find a way to leave the ashram, Jennifer would notice the guru peering at her through a keyhole, so she would open the door and find him standing there.

'I became rather scared of him, because he kept coming to my room at night.'

Another girl, 'Mary', would observe,

'He had a secret passageway from his house to the young girls' dormitory. Whoever he was carrying on with, he had switched to that dorm.'

Jennifer would add,

'He would come up anytime he wanted to and we would just

71

giggle. In the early days I never thought of him as having sexual desires. He was the guru . . .'

But Mary had talked to at least eight girls who had had sex with Muktananda.

'I knew that he had girls marching in and out of his bedroom all night long.'

In the States things were no different. When they were renovating a Miami hotel in 1979, Muktananda slept on the women's floor and invariably ordered that the youngest girls be put closest to his room. The door finally blew off in the lives of Chandra and Michael when they found out he had been molesting a thirteen-year-old girl whom the parents had entrusted to the ashram. And soon Stan Trout's open letter would blow the horn on this event. By then, Stan would have experienced a number of severe beatings through the ashram 'enforcers'. These beatings were ordered by the guru to keep Stan humble. Stan became a little stumbled when he learned that the guru had guns around the ashram. He defected permanently in 1981. His letter would explain why.

'When I left Muktananda's service, I did so because I had just learned of the threatening action he had taken against some of his long-term devotees who had recently left his service. He had sent two of his bodyguards to deliver threats to two young married women who had been speaking to others of Muktananda's sexual liaisons with a number of young girls in his ashram. It was immediately clear to me that I could not represent a guru who was not only taking sexual advantage of his female devotees but was threatening with bodily harm those who revealed the truth about him.'

This was heavy stuff from the former director of the Muktananda ashram.

Yet there remained another mystery. None of these people ever denied for a moment the reality of Muktananda's power. What baffled them was the extent of his power in the face of what could only be seen as evil episodes. It was a baffling pattern. Supernatural occult power and yet a lack of moral perfection. Claims of deity, godhood, while engaging in a kind of spiritual vampirism. As things stood, they had anything but a closed book. Michael Dinga would remark long after leaving the Indian

72

god-man,

'He put out a force field around him. You could palpably feel the force coming off him. It gave me the feeling I had latched on to something that would answer my questions.'

They all spoke of a kind of deep light that Muktananda's eyes gave off.

In 1982 Muktananda had a severe heart attack and died. Exactly what vehicle the Shakti Power, Kundalini, went to is not certain. But whereas Muktananda's 'Tantric' experiments were cloistered and hidden, not so with Acharya Rajneesh. Here was a god-man who did not hide behind anything. The alchemy of Rajneesh, meanwhile, would work on his minions as the substance of their souls went through rapid changes. There had to be a pattern in this somewhere. And in 1981 I would go to the Rajneesh ashram in Poona, India, to take a long, hard look. That trip would be my third trip to India in ten years. It would also coincide with the up-and-coming paperback edition of my second book that I worked on in Delhi while they were filming the motion picture, *Gandhi*.

11
RAJNEESH
THE AMBER CITY OF
THE GODS

We blasted down the mountains of Maharashtra towards Poona in a massive red diesel truck. It belonged to Martyn, a German friend. He had been in India and Nepal seven years and knew the roads of India as few Westerners do. We moved from mountain scenery to the denser heat of the plateau. His wife and child rode with him in the cabin. I was doing what I have wanted to do in India for over a decade—I sat on a deck chair clamped down to a specially-made balcony on the truck's roof. Perhaps in sunglasses and sipping tea in a mug I looked like a movie director. From fifteen feet up, a giraffe's aspect on the roads of India, my view was enviable.

We had decided to take the roundabout route from Bombay, passing timeless Indian villages nestled on rivers in Maharashtra. We beheld silhouetted forms praying and bathing in the rivers, temples jutting up into the clear sky, right out of the perennial land of the Vedas. On the roadside, the ancient world moved beneath us—water buffalo and cowherds, peasants carrying straw on their heads, women in bright saris, glistening in the sun. And mountain ridges rose up, carved ancient faces, all throwing the setting back two or three thousand years.

We picnicked in a field, watching the Maharashtran peasants gather hay. We watched from the roof loft. But I was tense inside about Poona; all did not sit well. Back on the road it ran through my mind.

I was bothered by a number of recent events in particular—a night with a Dutch diplomat in Bombay who was haunted by how his countrymen disappeared once they came under the tentacles of Rajneesh in Poona. Then there was a mangled German girl in a hospital in Goa with her own horror story, and countless other perceptions that had added up over the years. I also had an added perspective of all this from my own years in India under Sai Baba, and some of the things—call them secrets—that I discovered. Words of Jesus flooded my mind, 'You will know them by their fruits.'

I had come to India following two years of touring Europe and Britain speaking at various universities and gatherings on the subject of the Eastern gurus and an alternative view of what was really going on.

One thing struck me halfway through the tour. It was alarming how much impact Rajneesh was having in Europe, especially in Germany, Holland, and Denmark. Rajneesh centers were sprouting up everywhere, and sannyasins in red robes glowed on the streets of Europe. Amsterdam was flooded with them. And posters bearing the devilish, serpent-like face of Rajneesh were glued to the store windows and weathered brick walls of countless European cities. *Stern* magazine and *Der Spiegel* magazine of Germany had featured Rajneesh countless times in cover stories, often with color photos of sannyasins swaying in nude ecstasy in encounter groups, or doing things even more radical. Invariably, there was a haunting quality about Rajneesh's face, wherever it appeared. Its eyes kind of oozed out of various magazine covers and wall posters.

In the late afternoon of that early spring day in India, it was warm, aromatic, and breezy, as our huge West German diesel truck rolled ostentatiously into Poona. The truck was red, so the residents gathered that this was another Rajneesh event, that here was yet another group of anarchic sannyasins rolling in from some hideaway. Who knows what atrocities we had committed, they might think to themselves, sucking the motherland dry for our pleasure. And now we were here to draw from the pleasures of Poona. But after a second look at us, their eyes might almost look relieved. We were dressed in regular street wear, unlike the sannyasins in their fiery red robes and beads with Rajneesh's picture hanging at the bottom. And we did look different. After all I was up on the truck-roof enclosure staring down from fifteen feet up on my deck chair. It was a great way to photograph the setting.

We headed through the upper-class cantonment area where so many Britishers had lived and where so many of Poona's wealthy industrial class reside. For India it was impressive. Indeed Poona ranked with Bangalore as being among India's few pleasant cities in terms of weather and layout. It was elevated, drier and cooler than Bombay. And it did not have the incredible throngs of the poor and dying that the really big Indian cities like Madras and Calcutta had. We passed decent-looking Chinese restaurants, outdoor grills, cola stands. Then there were well-stocked merchant marts, clothing stores. Indeed, as I saw Poona roll by, I realized how well-appointed it was. Where else could Rajneesh and his entourage live? For India it was wealthy. It also had the entire range of indulgence that is on the menu of the sannyasin diet. I remembered how sparse things were when I was in Andhra Pradesh those years under Sai Baba. A trip into Bangalore then was a rare treat. These were full-fledged gourmands, meat-eaters, movie-goers, pleasure-seekers. For the Indian path this was indeed a novelty.

For everywhere my eyes went, I saw evidence of the mounting red tide. More and more sannyasins in their red robes fell into view. They stood out. They were fascinating. The local Indians gawked, stared, scorned underneath. They flirted with the European women, braless breasts flapping beneath the airy thin robes. Indeed, the locals lusted like mad. I tried not to lust myself. There was an incredible sensual aroma seeping through them, these red initiates.

And as we neared Koregeon Park, we did not need directions. We merely needed to note the body count of the sannyasins, mounting and mounting, everywhere. It was a white-man's takeover of an Indian city. They strolled holding hands, rubbing one another's backs, fondling each other with familiar ease. They emerged from stores and pavilions eating ice-cream cones, or mutton kebabs, or with bags of merchandise. They were big spenders and the locals were having a bonanza. India would cater for them, no matter what they did or did not wear, as long as they were big-time spenders. And the local merchants had learned how to play their game, while appearing tolerant.

We passed by the British-built Poona railway station, entering that sector of Poona where lies Koregeon Park, one of Poona's most fashionable districts. Modern movie houses whizzed by. Racing us and passing us in traffic were the sannyasins, riding their own motorcycles and scooters, women holding on from the back and laughing, the guys, *Swamis*, dare-deviling it through thick Indian traffic. Fearless, mocking. Some of them were 'hard customers, mean dudes'. No little wog was going to get in their way—they owned Poona, they and their Bhagavan, God, 'Sir God' as his name declares (*Bhagavan Sri*). On their motorcycles they were impatient, imperious, hostile with the local riff-raff, the native Poonaites. No one should dare impede them, or block their path. It reminded me of the old Maharajas on their elephants and caravans, commanding their servants to kick anybody in the way into the roadside gutter.

And like fireflies in Walt Disney's *Fantasia*, rickshaws, covered-wagon motorscooters, ushered the sannyasins out into the exotic Indian night of Poona as they rushed hither and yon in their little open chariots, laughing, gods on the verge of becoming God. It was twilight. City lights coming on, yet an amber sky to guide our path. Red, the sky was, Rajneesh red—perhaps Rajneesh's little cosmic event, his imprimatur on the sky to token his possession of the region. A poetic hint. But onwards the rickshaws sped, carrying two and three sannyasins, male and female. Some with exclusively female passengers—young, vital, pretty, sensual, well-bathed, oiled or scented, charging out into the pungent night air, maybe to a Japanese restaurant or ganja shop. Adding to this impression were whiffs of incense as we passed different roadside stalls burning bunches of sandalwood, jasmine, and rose incense.

We passed the Blue Diamond Hotel, a four- or five-star hotel, almost exclusively inhabited by the wealthier sannyasins. I could see clusters of them moving about in the foyer. The dining room glowed red. I was reminded that the average age of the sannyasins was early to mid-thirties.

We were in the Koregeon Park area. The houses were now larger, many of them estate houses. Large fences, gates, drives, even hedges surrounded them—rare for India. They had gardens, lawns, rose bushes and other flora, a greater rarity for India. Within a few blocks of Rajneesh's ashram, which stretched across numerous acres of Koregeon Park, were several thriving

77

cafes and restaurants, brimming with sannyasins. One had out-door tables, bamboo fencing, candles on the tables and stands. I detected whiffs of marijuana and hashish. Figures hunched over or leaning back, laughing, joking, amid raucous yells and laughter. Waiters being screamed at.

'It's a zoo,' I whispered down to Martyn through the truck roof.

We parked a few blocks away from the main gate in a nice open area under a large tree. That evening we would get a feel for the area, recover from the long ride, and eat at the bamboo res-taurant. Over mutton byrianis and assorted curries, we could observe them carrying on at neighboring tables in the large outdoor dining area. What kept mounting in my mind was the sheer feeling that these people gave off—a kind of alien spiritual aroma, a strange herbal mixture indeed. The common parlance for it was 'vibes'. Raucous laughs and pandemonium outside was endless as rickshaws would bring more of them to the restaurant or take them wherever they wanted to go.

We would end up spending the night in another area of Poona, Salisbury Park, another elite district, but free from the flood of inescapable vibes, that were strange, odd, haunting and that clung to everything in Koregeon Park. We were in the compound of friends of whom I had known before. Their fenced-in estate gently ushered in the night in silence, away from everything. Groves of mango trees wafted the night air with an aromatic fragrance. It all reminded me of my perennial love-hate relation-ship with India, now going on thirteen years of coming and going.

12

THE RAJNEESH ASHRAM OF POONA

If one studies the cosmic camps of different 'Enlightened Beings', their object has always been to concentrate their energy, forces, and power, to replicate themselves before they die.

The goal has always been a kind of nuclear fission of higher consciousness. But it has never fully worked. Rarely has there been a fit successor, a 'vehicle'. Cancer killed Ramanah Maharshi, cancer killed Ramakrishna, Meher Baba was rendered ineffective after a car accident, to give a few examples. And Muktananda recently vanished from the horizon with no one of any convincing stature to take his place. The gurus might leave behind one disciple at best who was 'close to the mark', but rarely did they have the same potency, and if they did (as in the case of Vivekananda, the premier disciple of Ramakrishna), then that one would die without another vehicle to take the fire, and the fire would die out, leaving an institution or a foundation.

The whole object of the New Age has been to have a mass enlightenment. A global cosmic event that would shift the tide of human history. In the light of this, Rajneesh has entered the race. His goal—to have a nucleus of 'Enlightened' people who would infiltrate the world. But he would be the Salvador Dali of gurus—a madman, a total eclectic, heedless of convention or morality. No double-standards or morality like Muktananda. With Rajneesh, anything goes.

But was this stuff really new? Twentieth century anarchy? No, it was as ancient as the Tantrics of north India. But it has not really been able to emerge on this scale until today. As Rajneesh had declared on numerous postcards that the ashram manufactured, they were conducting an original experiment, 'An Experiment in Provoking God'.

These things Martyn, Ada, and I had discussed often during our trip to Poona. And we went over it again our first night there.

The effects of Poona can be felt across much of India like the rumbles of an earthquake. Controversial rumors and reports emerge like war stories. Meanwhile, Rajneesh has flooded Indian magazines and papers for years. I had watched his ascent from afar for most of that time. For years I had some very strong inklings about how he operated and what was going on. But recent experiences in Goa and Bombay were even more chilling.

Before what was to become a long season in Poona I was with Martyn and Ada in Goa, the tropical Indian beach state between Bombay and Kerala. Goa is the infamous hippie beach haven that has become a sore spot with the Indian populace due to the scandalous carryings-on of the hippies and the inevitable adverse press coverage. Martyn and Ada had at one time been a part of that community, but recently they had left all that behind. For a while they had worked with a constructive outreach program in Goa known as Dilaram House. The staff were mostly ex-hippies who had been into heavy drugs but who had cleaned up their lives, now reaching out to the community.

Uli Kohler, head of Dilaram House in Goa, had at one time been a heroin addict, almost dying in Kabul with a rusty 'spike' in his arm. He had undergone a miraculous healing. Uli had been a German Communist. Now he was a Christian. And those who saw him from his old days almost could not believe the change. Uli referred us to a German girl he was worried about. She was in a hospital ward in Panjim, the nearby capital of Goa. For weeks the girl had been half-dead and almost incoherent.

The Rajneesh sannyasins of Goa, where many go when they are not in Poona with Rajneesh, had formed a community at Anjuna beach that had a reputation for violence and orgies and drugs. The local Indians hated them even more than they hated and distrusted the general colonies of hippies.

At the Anjuna beach flea-market, a large open-aired fiasco, Martyn and I got a certain amount of information on the girl. When we finally saw her at the hospital the effect was eerie and depressing. She had lost all will to live, she did not want to go home, and huge bleeding lesions ate halfway through her legs, which had been snapped like pretzels after she had been tossed

80

over a cliff. She was a paper-thin waif, bone-white. The staff were forced to tie her to the bed to keep her from picking at the deep running sores.

We spent hours with her. Among other things, we had to convince her to get out of India and go back to Germany. Otherwise it looked like she would die over there. She was terrified to talk. And among other things, we had to hunt down her passport which she had left with a tea-stall owner on one of the beaches. She would not give us her name. But eventually a few fragments of her story came out. Martyn coaxed her gently in German.

The story that emerged had the flavor of the occult movie, *Rosemary's Baby*. She had been one of many hangers-on to the Rajneesh community of mixed Europeans and Americans. Literally, it was an anything-goes situation. Their aim was to blow the roof off conventional morality. And that meant that there were experiments and victims. And this fragile girl had been a victim, a pathetic broken bird of a creature. What kept getting to us was the intense fear in her, and her silence.

It was already common knowledge that she had been forced into a gang rape after group members had a nude 'assault encounter'. They were soaring on a number of drugs, among them LSD. It was a full moon. 'A perfect time for witchcraft,' an observer of such events later commented. As a mad force drove the group, snarling and chortling, a number of them swung her over the cliff side in the moonlight. Back-and-forth, back-and-forth, they swung her, in the manner people at a party swing someone before pitching them into a swimming pool. Except this was a cliff. She wailed and they laughed. Finally they pitched her and left her for dead, heading back to their cabins. Fortunately, she missed the really big rocks and landed, in the main, on the sand. Otherwise she would have been dead for sure.

But other things had transpired and she refused to talk about them. Were these Rajneesh disciples outcasts from Poona experimenting with the ultimate in barbarism? 'No,' she told us. She had been to Poona and had met them there. Many of them often came and went between Poona and the Goa community. Had she met Rajneesh? 'Yes.' Up until the violent incident, she was waiting to return to Poona and be initiated. At that point we could get no more out of her. Later I heard that she was flown back to Germany. By then I would be in Poona finding 'an enigma within a riddle within a puzzle'.

Then when we were in Bombay, immediately before our trip to Poona, another sobering event occurred. One night I was with an old friend, Ray, a resident of India of some forty years, when he suddenly got an urgent phone call. We were immediately summoned to go out to Bombay's Hotel Intercontinental to have a private meeting with one of the top officers in the Dutch consulate. He and some of the other European consuls had known about me from my books. This was a first contact, and the Dutch official was representing the other European consuls informally. For forty minutes he squirmed in his lounge chair in the expensive suite, probing endlessly into the various odd practices of Indian mystics and then asking how Rajneesh fits into the picture. Finally he got to what was really at issue.

Sweating from Bombay's fiery humidity forever seeping through everything, even the air-conditioning of this expensive hotel, the Dutchman told us,

'For several years now, I cannot begin to tell you how many calls we have had from Europe to check on this person or that person who 'disappeared', or fell out of communication. Or formal requests asking us to check the whereabouts of various people. Or people whose visa is long-expired. Whatever the cause, the alarming thing is that we often have to go up to Poona, as we are obliged to do in the formality of having physically to repatriate someone, whether they are sick, penniless, or have been institutionalized for psychiatric reasons. When we do this, we encounter, far too often, the fact that there is no record for that person, and for all intents and purposes, he or she has just plain disappeared. Disappeared from the face of the earth. You can talk to these other sannyasins, the Rajneesh followers in the red robes, and they just will not tell you anything. They play dumb. They toy with you or insult you.

'But now it is reaching a crisis, and my office and the other European consulates, and this includes the consulates of Canada and Australia as well, have checked with one another and we have all run into the identical problem. It is unbelievable. Now we are forming a coalition and we have begun to exert great force on the Indian government.'

He turned to me and said,

'Would you advise us? If I get the other consuls together, could you speak to us as a group, and give us some idea as to what is happening with these people? Are they being murdered in ritual murders? What is happening?'

He was utterly bewildered and incredulous, and confessed to being way out of his league as far as spiritual things went, especially Eastern beliefs, not to mention the teachings of Rajneesh.

The Dutchman confessed his inability to see into the mystery of Poona.

'What impels people to go to Poona and stay there under Rajneesh? How can they put up with it? Why don't they see through it? People from good families, influential Europeans, very wealthy and influential people.'

What made things very difficult for the embassies was that all ashram records of people were private and off-limits and were open to no one. Compounding this was the fact that without these records it was almost impossible to correlate the new names given by Rajneesh with the original family names. Forgetting their old names was a means for the initiates of burying their old identities. And they rarely knew each other's family names. The ashram meanwhile seemed to hold all of the local Poona authorities in its grip, and was intimated by no one and no governmental power.

But tangible evidence of death and disappearance cropped up often enough to make the case almost ironclad. Death of the super-famous was a lot harder to obscure. The Dutch diplomat cited the most recent case, that of Prince Welf of Hanover, Germany, a nephew of Queen Elizabeth of England, roughly the age of Prince Charles, who was initiated under Rajneesh along with his wife and daughter and given an Indian name (Swami Anand Vimalkirti). He moved to Poona. Then one of many diplomatic traumas took place. The prince was killed in one of Rajneesh's closed groups and the body was then burned before an autopsy could be performed.

'Someone thirty-three years old doesn't just die!' said the Dutchman. 'If they can't trace the cause of death of a German

83

prince, if the Indian authorities don't step into an accident this great, how about all of the other ordinary people who disappear!'

The entire ashram had celebrated at the time when the body of the prince was consumed in the flames of the open pyre. Looking on were the prince's distraught relatives.

We agreed with the Dutch diplomat, this was a diplomatic crisis, indeed an international crisis. And they had to use their diplomatic clout to get the Indian government to act fast—the Dutch consulate in league with the other European, Australian, and Canadian consulates. I agreed to address the group if I had time, and look up the people in Poona whom he suggested I see for an inside look.

Meanwhile he assured me that his consulate, like all the other consulates, had searched India for the missing persons—from hotel records to checks cashed. And almost invariably the last region to be traced before loss of contact was Poona. Friends and relatives back home often had letters postmarked Poona, often with written references to this amazing new find, the Rajneesh ashram.

Then again in Poona there were the local hospital records of people forced to use their legal names (passport verifiable in the registry) who had been sent by the ashram. But after they were eventually released, many would then disappear! Those from this group, whom the consulates had tracked down and found through the hospitals, were often insane or severely damaged physically (as in the common reports of attempted suicide). They also learned from a number of private physicians that the Rajneesh ashram had pressured the local hospitals, especially the Poona asylum, not to divulge any information about its sannyasins. Inquiry was now close to impossible. The consulates learned that it was now exceedingly difficult to gain entrance into the asylum to look for or visit those after whom they were inquiring (as I found out myself).

You could say then that Martyn, Ada, and I, that first night in Poona, were anything but disinterested observers. We felt a quiet alarm blended with a controlled fury. Martyn and Ada had also heard reports that numerous German and Scandinavian friends, from their old beach era in Goa, were now caught in the web of Rajneesh. They spoke of this as we sat on the truck-roof enclosure and sipped jasmine tea.

In a sense, the truck paralleled the changes in their own lives. They had lived and travelled in the massive diesel truck for seven years, going between Nepal and India. Invariably pushing drugs was a part of this enterprise. Formerly Martyn brought with him a huge loin-clothed Shivaite yogi with matted hair, who would sleep near him and his family in the van. Now the van was cleaned up and all the Tibetan Tankas and pictures of Indian gods were off the walls. Martyn had a well-deserved reputation among the long-termers in India for being a 'heavy-weight'. Now they would be equally as baffled by his compassion and generosity. Yet how we would all hold up under the immense weight of Poona I was not sure.

13

KOREGEON PARK LIVE

We trucked back to Koregeon Park in the early morning hours, attempting to reach the huge front gates before they closed for Rajneesh's morning discourse at Buddha Hall. I was nervous, wary. My head buzzed from meager sleep, Poona mosquitos, and early-morning Mysore coffee.

We parked a block from the crowded front gate. I felt very ostentatious. The truck took up half the street. It reminded me of an amphibious truck or a tank. And I was beginning to feel like a Western gunslinger, ready for action, walking into Dodge City, passing quiet but explosive saloons.

Much of the crowd turned to watch us emerge from the truck. We were being 'vibed-out'. It was the old psychic doberman-pinscher routine. I knew it well. Were we enemy, or were we among the endless stream of naive seekers stumbling in to see their god? This was the outer layer of the onion. In any spiritual hierarchy there are those who glory in merely being able to stand at the gate and gawk at new arrivals. When I was in Sai Baba's inner circle, I would look down my nose twenty onion layers at those who gawked at newer arrivals than they. My interest, ultimately, would be to probe the inner circle, the central core of Rajneesh's cryptic universe, where his real objectives were being worked out. The gawkers would have about as much access to this as the tourists. Indeed, the medium level initiates, I knew from experience, would not have an inkling.

From an intuitive sense of smell, and evidence I had gathered, I was gripped by the feeling that herein was a maze and only a few made it to the inner chambers, past all the cryptic signs, dead-ends, tests, and barriers. Rajneesh had partitioned his kingdom like the Emperor of Constantinople: his hierarchies were compartmentalized such that only a trusted few knew what was really happening in the kingdom. The artisans were isolated from the

86

priesthood, the military were isolated from the palace guard, the intelligentsia were sequestered to another domain, away from other executors, other staff, others with limited power.

It was an ancient concept—used today from the Masons to the KGB—where intermediaries and aspirants had no clue as to the true nature of what was going on, from the ultimate core of activity to the final goals. There was a distracting cornucopia within, something for everybody, so that whatever you happened to grab onto, now you 'knew the answer'. The god within the gates had carefully covered the ground, freeing himself from the burden of consistency. Laws and teachings could be changed with a wave of the hand.

The massive carved-oak front gate with the huge bolts and swinging doors was called 'the gateless gate', by 'the Master'. The doors, in oriental motif, were standing symbols of this cryptic kingdom. Forbidding, palatial, it was a medieval kingdom gate. And like the spiritual realms in a Tibetan temple painting, a Tanka, on the outside of the gates armed guards stood menacingly. It was a contradiction, for here were two messages being communicated: anarchy—all is permitted, the standard Rajneesh trademark; but also, overlaying this, caution, total control, distrust, paranoia. It was very 'uptight', to use their jargon. Rajneesh had told them, 'This is not a democracy.' Indeed, he supplied them with the forewarning, 'This is a dictatorship.' If all is permitted, turn it around, and realize that all is permitted to the ruler as well.

There is a lot happening at one time at the gate. And I am trying to take it all in. The guards scrutinize each visitor, continually fingering their large West German billy-clubs of hard rubber. My friend points out that there are stun guns within them, or stun prods. Enough to knock you down. These instruments trigger my memory of three sickly looking specimens who walked by me weeks back at the Victoria railway station in Bombay. Each of these sannyasins babbled effeminately, gesturing with thin white arms. But the visual obscenity of the moment were the plaster casts covering the entire crowns of their heads. At the time I sensed that they seemed to glory in their humiliation. But I wondered then, 'Why are there so many Rajneesh followers in bandages? What exactly is going on?'

Waves and waves pour through the gates like amber flames. The tide of red initiates skip and jubilate. They all have 'the knowing vibe'; they are privy. It is a controlled ecstasy. Those not wearing the sannyasin robes are deeply scrutinized. Several ahead of us fail to make it through. The guard seems to know them. He looks as though he would enjoy doing some damage, maybe going for a home run with one of the heads. The eyes are fierce. Maybe a little sadistic. Two of the non-sannyasins turned away get the point. They don't bother arguing. After all, it is not their place. But they come off as losers, unworthy, second-rate seekers. One reason that they are second-rate is that they obviously don't have any money. And it costs to hear god speak every morning. Ten rupees. Looking at their clothes, it is also doubtful that they are clean enough to get into Buddha Hall where Rajneesh is due to appear.

Now a sannyasin is held back from entering. He sort of whines an 'aw . . . gee, this is unfair'. The guard is a big German. He looks down at the wimp. It is obvious what he would enjoy doing. The wimp now needs to be assured that he counts. He needs babying, but this is a pretty hard crew moving through the gates. Hardened emotionally. Not too much sympathy. He is looking for someone to assure him of his, to use a contemporary phrase, 'personhood'. He does not look like a survivor. He's a weak weed. As we move nearby, an obese woman is droning in his ear. He is nodding weakly. The guard looks on. The weak weed looks as though he has eaten a lot of yogurt over the years and stood in a lot of protest lines. People had their rights, he had his rights. Now his rights were being violated.

But the corpulent woman in the balloon sannyasin dress had the answer from an open magazine with a discourse given by 'Swami'. Her voice was droning the substance of the article in his ear. I would get a copy later just to check it out to see if my ears were really hearing what I was hearing. Indeed, I would get a lot of material. To quote her quoting 'Swami' Rajneesh, about sannyasins being denied entrance at the gate,

'Whatsoever happens in this commune happens according to me . . . You are nobody to judge what is right and what is wrong. If you know it already, you are not needed here. You have become enlightened—go home . . . This is none of your business—to decide what is just and what is unjust. This is not an ordinary place, so ordinary things won't apply here. Some extraordinary experiment is on . . . It is not an ordinary place; everything is looked after. And if somebody needs a hit on the head, he is given it. You should not prevent it, otherwise you will be coming into his growth too, and you will hinder him and you will be hindering yourself . . . The moment you become part of my commune you leave everything to me. Otherwise work will become impossible.'

The wimpy sannyasin was nodding weakly while she droned on. He was beginning to see the light. I stood nearby listening.

'There are some foolish people who have renounced their sannyas because they saw something unjust being done. Now they're just losing their opportunity. It was not their business; you have to come here for your own growth. This acceptance has to be total—only then is work possible, only then can I help you . . . This is not going to be a democracy. You are not to be asked what should be done and what should not be done. This should be remembered from the very beginning—that this is not going to be a democracy. Your votes will never be taken. You become part of it with that knowledge—that whatsoever I decide is absolute. If you don't choose that way, you are perfectly happy to leave.'[1]

He had his choice, and he ambled off obediently. He would try again the next day. He would keep trying until he was allowed to enter.

I camouflaged myself in the group flow, tuning down my high intensity within. I looked into the guard's eyes implacably, fully expecting entrance. I oozed right by him in the flow. There were other guards on the inside of the gate, and various alert, authoritative eyes belonging to sannyasins of high rank who were motioning directions. One surly Indian woman nodded to someone in the crowd to go straight down the central street and leave any belongings in the locker department. I moved as though I knew the protocol, watching carefully for procedure.

I felt quietly relieved that we had made it through in our street dress. But I masked any emotional reaction. I did not even want to swallow. The momentum had to continue in the things-as-usual fashion. There was definitely a profound sense of surveillance everywhere. A strong sense of caution, of uptightness. The mood was violin-string tight. The line of guards on the inside of the gate looked coiled up enough to unleash at any moment. A sneeze and one of these zombie-sannyasins would get wasted with a billy-club. It resembled a punk rock band on stage sneering at the audience. Just waiting for 'a little agro', as they say in London ('agr-o-vation').

Buddha Hall was left of the gate, so we first had to detour down the central street to the storage department, where we gave our wallets and watch to the girl who put them in a basket and gave us an elastic number tag. Next we had to walk through radar-gateways like the ones at international airports. Then we had to be body searched for guns or knives. Everyone was body searched, even their very own sannyasins. These were in long orderly lines. There was almost no talk. The herd of people moved like goats going to slaughter. At each checkpoint we moved closer to Buddha Hall, where Rajneesh was due to appear within the hour.

I had read about this entire routine in a piece by a very zealous Bernard Levin, in his feature column in *The Times* of London. It was amazing to find the normally caustic and erudite humanist Levin, who dispenses so deftly with the more 'pedestrian' religions, become so enthusiastic about Rajneesh. The self-appointed intelligentsia had indeed swallowed the whole camel. I wrote Levin an interesting letter.

So I was very much aware of the next checkpoint—the sniffing line. Everybody had to have their armpits and body sniffed by a very dedicated line of girls in red. Rajneesh could not tolerate any smells, especially colognes or perfumed soaps. 'God', it seemed, was highly allergic to various smells. He also had asthma. I noticed that several people were turned away at different checkpoints. Martyn and I had been forewarned, so we were well scrubbed with an odorless soap.

The final checkpoint was the shoe department, where again shoes were exchanged for tags. This was near the rim of the massive elliptical structure known as Buddha Hall where over three thousand would gather. It had wide stairs and an entrance-way with a series of guards whispering to people in commanding tones to be absolutely silent. Signs commanded the same thing.

The most prominent sign at the entrance to Buddha Hall read, 'Leave your minds and your slippers here'.

Buddha Hall was spotless. Way down in front was a stage with Rajneesh's throne. Nearby were pictures of him with piercing eyes. People had to stop at the entrance to be directed where to sit. Guards pointed to various sections. Hierarchy was evident. There were roped-off areas for various levels of initiates. The long-term devotees and ashram residents sat down at the very front. Everyone sat on the floor. Martyn and I were two-thirds of the way back. We were in an ocean of red. Standing near pillars at numerous posts were armed guards. There were various signs giving the rules. Silence was an absolute command. If anyone sneezed or coughed they would get a severe look. More than that and they would be motioned out of the hall. Anyone resisting a guard would get billy-clubbed.

We sat in pin-drop silence, three thousand of us, in an ocean of red. Minutes ticked by as a tense, controlled energy mounted. Expectation built up. People craned their heads frantically to try and sight 'Bhagavan' (God) first. The hush suddenly crackled with awe. Glinting in the distance was a slow-moving white Rolls Royce, purring around the perimeter of the hall on a privately built road. It was travelling the standard hundred yards from Rajneesh's front porch to his throne at Buddha Hall. His mansion was through a private gate deep within the ashram. It was called the Lao Tzu house. Rajneesh never left the premises. His outline could be seen through the tinted windows. One girl in front of me had been weeping uncontrollably for half an hour, her head in her boyfriend's lap. Now she was on her haunches peering about desperately just for a glimpse of him.

The air-conditioned Rolls Royce purred to a stop. A frantic silence covered us. Three thousand pairs of hands were raised in the prayer position in obeisance to Rajneesh. Women looked desperate just to touch him. Many eyes were tearful, beseeching. The girl in front started sobbing again. A nearby guard glared at her to stop, motioning the exit. She stopped. Rajneesh's personal bodyguard stood at the door of the Rolls Royce and opened it for him. He looked like a finely trained instrument of death, and would obliterate anyone who approached his master unsolicited. A tall Scot with a beard, he walked behind Rajneesh as his guru entered Buddha Hall at the front, over a hundred feet away from me. Rajneesh slowly moved to his throne, his hands in the *namaste* prayer position, as he pivoted slowly to face his entire audience. The hush was electric. One could just feel the guards psychically trying to control the surges passing across the audience, lest a tidal wave of emotion rip through the dam of enforced composure, and bodies hurtle and twist at the base of Rajneesh's stage in a panic just to touch the hem of his robe.

Rajneesh's body was a glove covering a naked force. The body was prematurely aged, wizened—he was fifty but looked seventy. He looked like a sorcerer in a Tolkien epic. A spell was in effect, no doubt about it. Here sat his human chattel, hors d'oeuvres on a tray, delicacies to be tasted, experimented on, transmuted—and for those few with the capacity and the drive, perhaps total explosion. These were his salmon all trying to scale the immense waterfall that he was setting before them. They had to be willing to dash their lives upon the rocks. I knew the ancient game well. I knew the complexities of gurudom. I myself had reached the eternal precipice, the leap where there is no turning back, ten years before in South India. The point of final oblivion, the void—I could smell it lurking in the hall like death.

I felt it with an intensity I had not felt since ten years before, when I was with Sai Baba. The scent, the odor, the feeling was here, there was no mistaking it—the guru-force, the symphony of seduction, the black hole reaching into the void in the center of the human form reclining back on his throne, watching out through serpent-like eyes. It did have a superhuman conscious-ness—but its origins and flavor were well disguised from this adoring and desperate throng.

A pinpoint of unspeakable grief began to emerge from within me, as I scanned these regressed, child-like adults. I had a special soft spot for the more vulnerable, sensitive, and attractive females. They were immediately lovable. But the process widened from there. I had seen a lot of faces that morning that looked like they were dying inside. I wanted to wrap my arms around scores of these girls and pull them to my chest, pro-tectively, and then somehow cross that gulf of communication and reach them.

'Eve, you're back in the garden. Yes, it all makes great sense, seductive sense. And yes, no doubt, that is a very attractive fruit indeed. But you see only half the picture. There is another picture on the other side of the explosion.'

And my younger brothers in the audience? I wanted to sit them down and stare deeply into their souls and soberly warn them.

But everybody here had made a choice, and that is how they got here—all of them, each one of them. It literally took a miracle to get me to see the figure-ground, and that happened when I was an advanced adept, more along the path than most of them would ever go.

Rajneesh began speaking . . . in Hindi. He alternated between Hindi and English, leapfrogging languages each month. There was a meager fraction of Indians even permitted in the Hall, so the words formed a monotonous drone that almost no one in the auditorium could understand. Water over the dam. But faces still looked 'knowing', as they fine-tuned to receive the higher spiritual message.

Over an hour passed. Without notice Rajneesh suddenly got up, headed for his Rolls Royce, and purred around the rest of the circular hall, passing near my section. Three thousand bodies pivoted in frozen adoration. My space was not in the currents of his 'Buddha-field'; it was a gap, a different energy by far. His window was parallel with me. Our eyes locked in a protracted silence—I had something to tell him. His head twisted away at the end of it.

What nobody in the audience knew, including me, was that within only a few weeks he would stop appearing for darshans. No one would know why. People would speculate that his endless battle with health problems was the cause of it. A month later headlines and full page ads across India would announce that 'Bhagavan' had taken a vow of silence and was beginning his final phase. I would be in Bangalore by then. Later I would return to Poona again for five or six visits lasting from days to a week or two each. By then the ashram would be in total up-heaval, while he appeared occasionally for a 'silent darshan'.

The hall let out and I felt relieved at the lessening of tension. In minutes I was sitting with Martyn on the main ashram avenue watching sannyasins flow like bees in a hive, in and out of boutiques, supply stores, snack bars, offices, the bookstore, post office, bathrooms, cabins and residences deep within the ashram. Or they would drift in New-World daze along roads, paths, or in the little private park.

Soon we explored the premises, a world of its own within India: spotless, manicured, hygienic, plush with flowers, bushes, ferns, trees—all immaculate and tended right down to the minute detail of flower combinations. The architecture was modern, with Japanese and Scandinavian influences predominant, creating an overall effect of immense comfort and security. It was a haven, an escape from India. They could emerge into the land of India, out of this cocoon, when they felt like it. Here on the ashram they were far from the probing eye of the public, or voyeuristic Indians whom many of them had learned to loathe. Here they were free, free to become liberated by any means conceivable. There were no rules except those of Rajneesh.

For India the huge walled-in Rajneesh ashram was the ultimate in utter affluence, tailored for Western tastes. And, of course, it had cost a fortune. They had imported entire kitchens from Switzerland and Germany. The Dutch and Swiss ran the bakery operations. The French added a creative touch to the main kitchen, turning out soufflés, quiches, and what not. Meals served only at five-star hotels for gourmet vegetarian tastes. Meat was not allowed, but liquor was. No dope on premises, but there was plenty outside—from cocaine to heroin. Pot and LSD were common fare. It was a sensualist's paradise. The dream of the hippie community of Goa but with the wealth to back it up. It was, to quote Rajneesh, his 'Buddha-field' where buddhas would one day be spawned in an experiment in mass enlightenment. He would do what the other masters had not been able to do, 'mediocre gods like Muktananda'. His laboratory for these experiments was formidable.

By lunch time Martyn and I could smell the ovens pouring forth the fumes of rich brownies, donuts, and pizza. Apparently these smells were permissible; there was not a long line of sniffers outside the kitchens. We succumbed, filling our trays in the largest cafeteria on the ashram, and then filtering outdoors to sit at a comfortable terrace table under an awning. We ate and watched. I studied face after face, probing, looking for hints and

94

signs of character, of background, and personality. And then signs of Rajneesh's chemistry. What I perceived was so intense I wanted to escape totally into my food and get lost in it. What I was picking up with my sensors was a terrible knowledge—a knowledge of what Rajneesh's wrecking-crews, his intense therapy groups, were bringing upon his subjects wandering by me and sitting next to me. I would hone in on these realities later—verifying what I perceived, in his recorded talks, and from some of his former subjects, some of them inner circle.

I studied wave after wave of red-gowned sannyasins passing through the cafeteria line. It was safe territory and permissible to look, to peer from my terrace table under the awning as I slowly drank one cup of coffee after another. Good coffee, I might add. Red, orange, purple, and ochre garb passed by me, tailored as dresses, robes, gowns, sweat-suits, bikinis, halter-tops, and shorts. Some of the bodies were practically nude in the Poona noontime heat. They mingled in a sensual aroma, bodies touching like flames.

They chattered at tables, super-hip, upbeat, in-the-know. Some sat in depersonalized, quasi-omniscient silence. Some carried themselves like gods. Others had dog tags around their necks stating that they were on probation or off-limits or in isolation or silence. Some drooped in pitiable self-deprecation, a wormy self-abasement that made Woody Allen look like a stud.

But they were all on a jet-propelled roller-coaster ride, whether they were gods or worms, or one thing today and another tomorrow. It was a communism of the soul, a blending in, a homogenization of very diverse types—movie stars, famous journalists, royalty, and aristocracy, esteemed intellectuals and the super-rich on the one hand, salt-and-peppered with Amsterdam prostitutes, Charles Manson psycho types, perverts of all varieties, Essalen types, San Fran gays, and a whole list of tarot readers and psychics. They were all blended together in a giant mixmaster. To repeat, there was a communistic lowest-common-denominator principle at work. But above that was the inescapable spiritual hierarchy in action. All were equal, but all were not equal. To quote Orwell's *Animal Farm*, 'Some were more equal than others'. They were scrambling to climb the

Rajneesh mountain, and all was fair in love and war, even standing on a few heads.

Martyn and I passed through the wide outside eating area, and by the indoor dining room to the main street. We decided to sit on a bench backed against a modern plate-glass office building on the main-street corner. It was the office of Vijaya Laxmi, Rajneesh's second-in-command who ran the ashram. She is a hated and feared woman who will do anything Rajneesh tells her. He has described her and the two other women in his chain of command as his 'three little witches'. Their pictures look it. They are ugly and ruthless-looking and utterly devoted to Rajneesh. He wants no male rivals, so he has set up the ashram functions as quasi-matriarchal, which is the model in Wicca (or witchcraft). Under the top man, come the women, then the other men.

Laxmi continually did the dirty work, whether it was ejecting people or bribing the local police. At that time she had been in Delhi for months, first trying to buy massive amounts of land in Gujarat. That fell through, the papers said, because of a bribe scandal. So now she was trying to buy the palace of a Maharaj in Chail, Simla. It would have more privacy than Poona, and in it 'Bhagavan' could really begin his heavy experiments, surrounded by a true medieval fortressed rock wall with an electric fence that they planned to put on top. The ashram guard was also being beefed up as more and more hefty male sannyasins were recruited and trained in kung fu, Tai Chi, karate, and Samurai swordsmanship.

Later that afternoon a red, high-energy tide of sannyasins suddenly flooded the streets of the ashram. The ashram glowed with secretive smiles and conspiratorial looks as people emerged from private meditation, primal scream, and Tao sessions, touch and massage encounters, and the famous Tantra Sex encounter. All morality was being obliterated. Underneath the excitement was a zombie-like boredom in some, a New-World daze. I strongly sensed a terrible, obscene, gaping wound underneath this facade—a collective lacerated psyche.

Soon it would be time to leave in the amber dusk of the late afternoon. Martyn and I would pass back out into the streets of Poona through the exclusive ashram gates. We had shown ourselves around enough for the entry guards to know us and let us back in without scrutiny. Outside the front gate, crowds and huddles of sannyasins spoke with a variety of foreign accents as they smoked. Smoking was prohibited on the premises.

As we walked back to the diesel truck we passed the sannyasins as they talked, emoted, mocked, hugged, interacted, transacted, and propositioned one another freely—anytime, anywhere. I couldn't wait to drive to another part of Poona—Salisbury Park, where we had set up our headquarters with a friend.

I was given a suite with a shower. And I longed to soap off that day's heat and tension, and unwind with Martyn and Ada in some Poona Chinese restaurant. We had plenty of time to learn the ropes, and we would. Martyn had spent hours that day talking to some of his German friends, and he had gathered a lot of information. At dinner we would be able to discuss this freely. At the ashram we had to appear ambivalent to them, so they would not know where we stood—at least for now. Because there was absolutely no denying the fact that we were being scrutinized by a weighty presence when we were within the gates of the Rajneesh ashram. Everyone there was part of 'the eye of Sauron'. It was the feeling of being watched I used to get as a youth, when I walked through the bazaars of Damascus or Cairo.

14

RECONNAISSANCE AT THE GOLDEN DRAGON

The day was so intense, I wanted to melt into oblivion over a hot pitcher of Chinese tea and a festive Mandarin platter. Martyn, Ada, and I lounged back at a large table in one of Poona's most fashionable Chinese restaurants. Here we hoped to recount, in a leisurely manner, what we had independently learned on the Rajneesh ashram. We felt more relaxed, having showered off Poona's warm humidity and grime and put on clean clothes. But the tense underlying sense of caution would not leave us alone. We were aliens and the membrane of surveillance, which had been around us on the ashram, was still faintly with us. As we had known then, and hoped would not be detected on the ashram, the 'light' within us was of a very different kind from the 'light' within them, the sannyasins.

Here at least we hoped to drop our guard and breathe freely. But there was no escape. The outer armor of impassivity which hid our revulsion throughout the day had to remain. The charged sense of what was at stake carried the cautious mood of a spy intrigue. Shades of Robert Ludlum.

Across the restaurant a 'Rajneesh event' was unfolding—an ever-present reminder of the sobering reality we were prying into. It had its own layers of ironies. A tall, raw-boned German, with fierce, impassioned eyes and a certain vulgar defiance, was what the Rajneeshies call 'love-bombing' with a lady who seemed to be an American Jewess. It was a thinly-veiled public display of eroticism. Such behavior is not well received in India, where they even censor kissing from their films, and where Indians virtually never display public affection, even between man and wife. They become either voyeuristic or indignant when foreign public displays are forced upon them. And here was a classic. I felt apologetic for my culture as did Martyn for his. The two sannyasins were oblivious and indifferent to their effect on the people forced to watch them in the restaurant as their activities became an uncomfortable spotlight.

Steamy-eyed kisses, giggles, lewd innuendo, mocking laughter, and foot activity under the table ensued. An exploring hand here, a nudging foot there, for all the natives to see. Finally I glared at the German severely. So did Martyn. I noticed Martyn in a rock-like crossbeam glare with the defiant German. Martyn had an incredibly tough background, and it was in his eyes. The other German backed down when Martyn said something to him in German. A change had come into Martyn's life, however, and it was unlikely he would resort to his old tactics, such as crow-baring the guy through the window. No, this was a new Martyn; he had softened incredibly. Ada whispered to me through a smile that this new mellowness was unheard of in Martyn's old days. But the other guy knew he should not try to take Martyn on. And soon the two sannyasins left, swaggering out of the restaurant with palms on each other's posteriors. Martyn shook his head sadly.

'Love-bombing!' we all announced with a can-you-believe-it look. What is love-bombing? Its beginnings come from Essalen-type groups where you disgorge your deepest secrets into the middle of a marathon encounter group of total strangers who by the end know your psyche intimately. They have chewed and traumatized their way through your deepest games, fears, and defenses. Now they can approach you in total love and familiarity. This becomes a form of universal body language as you learn to love the world, now that you are privy to the secrets of the human psyche. When encounter-group graduates meet each other on the streets of Berkeley or New York or wherever, the look is an oozing, sincere, desperate look of total intimacy, at times flavored with a kind of glee. What is amazing is that it is often done with near-total strangers.

Picture the look, if you will, of Humphrey Bogart and Lauren Bacall eyeing each other's souls for the last time at the Kiev Railroad Station before a grand archetypal departure. This is the intensity. Now picture the Rajneesh ashram and the streets now aswarm with this privy form of communication. You are walking down the streets of Poona, two adult-kids in red smocks glow from half a block away as they approach each other. They may not have met beyond a few passing words in the cafeteria. But never mind, suddenly it is Ryan O'Neal and Ali McGraw in *Love Story*. When they part, they will have love-bombed. When they are next in each other's proximity, they may be love-bombing other people, even ignoring one another. Here is the bargain—'total intimacy' with the freedom of no strings attached. But as we learned, that too has a certain price tag. It does wonders for people's feeling of security. Here is romantic pantheism operating at its best where those special little feelings are now for the cosmos-at-large. Emotional hyper-inflation.

But that was only the surface layer of the onion.

'I talked to some of my German friends from Goa today. They have taken initiation,' Martyn said, in a low voice.

He had spent hours that afternoon talking with them while I was doing a little looking around on my own. I had spent hours in the ultra-modern bookstore where they had most of Rajneesh's 350 books, and stacks of the ashram magazine, *Sannyas*. This periodical quotes Rajneesh more brazenly than many of the books and interviews which the ashram Public Relations department releases to the public after careful editing. I bought a large stack of the magazines, which were expensive glossy affairs with color photos and Western sophistication. That was part of my factfinding contribution for the evening. But I was anxious to hear Martyn and Ada.

Martyn looked pained.

'One couple I knew a few years before in Goa have really changed. They were from Bremen, wealthy people. Rajneesh isn't interested if you don't have the money. He gave them sannyas initiation with the new names and the beads. Immediately the guy had to get a vasectomy, sterilization. And when they found out she was pregnant, they ordered her to go for an abortion at their health clinic. Sterilization is almost always required now if you want to be a sannyasin. Rajneesh is against the family, against marriage. That is why almost all the married couples are told to separate and find new partners. Even their children they are required to throw away, give up, make common property of the commune, the ashram. I found out that some of the white children that are found begging on the streets of Poona are Rajneesh throwaways. They say they are liberated from the *karma*, the responsibility of their kids. That the kids get in the way of their . . . how do you say . . . freedom to sexuality.'

Martyn was struggling hard to put it in the right English.

'Well they did an abortion on her. They did a real sloppy job on her and she almost died, she told me. But she said she could feel Bhagavan with her through it. Sure! At any rate they say they are happier than ever before. I asked them about a few of the deaths of some of the Germans around. And they said, "Sure, accidents will happen. We are playing for high stakes. Some people don't have what it takes, they fall apart. There are many casualties. But they shouldn't be here." They had hardened even more than before when I knew them in Goa. No conscience, none at all.

'Rajneesh says that only the wealthy can afford to be spiritual—only they have the energy and time,' Martyn continued.

I recalled the oft-quoted saying of Rajneesh,

'If you have squeezed the whole juice of life, death will be the ultimate orgasm.'

'How about those without money so the joy ride can continue?'

Simple. There was an influx of high-class Western call girls in Bombay, most of them sannyasins out to get more money. The fellows usually resorted to dope smuggling, going as far as Bangkok and the Golden Triangle. Poona papers had run steady reports of British dope busts of sannyasins at Heathrow airport, and busts in Amsterdam. Rajneesh had given them his distant kiss of approval, but with public disavowal. Some of the Rajneeshies going to Goa were orchestrating a sophisticated dope trail on native fishing boats.

Living on the high-track had big stakes. The wife of one of Martyn's friends was presently in the local asylum. They had split up, the ex-husband had told Martyn nonchalantly. Here surfaced the common attitude, a hard, ruthless indifference to one another's misfortune. There were some devastating problems and a helping hand was rare. Total aloneness. As Rajneesh had said,

'Zen is not concerned with your state of mind. It has no desire to nourish it any more . . . Hence it has no idea of God—no father in the sky. It leaves you totally alone because only in aloneness is maturity possible. It leaves you totally in insecurity.

It gives you no security, no guarantee . . . And that is what sannyas is also: a quantum leap into insecurity, a quantum leap into the unknown.'[1]

The human by-product of this could be seen at the local Poona asylum. Martyn had talked earlier to the German consulate in Bombay, and they told him that on the average they had personally to appear in Poona to repatriate fifty to sixty cases per year from the local asylum. Very alone people. The ashram, meanwhile, would brutally sever its prior association with flunkies. People wailing at the gate for mercy were not uncommon, as former love-bombers would pass them by.

Martyn leaned across the table.

'Rajneesh has an X-rated tape going around Bombay. He will say anything. One section has him slowly reciting all the four-letter words ending them with his hissing sound. F . . . F . . . F . . . , just like a mantra. I heard part of it. His jokes are unbelievable.'

The touchy ones were the anti-Semitic ones. Indeed there was a strange chemistry going on at the ashram.

'Thirty to forty percent are Jews according to the ashram census. And there are also many, many Germans. Rajneesh has told them that the people he admires most in history are Alexander the Great, Joseph Stalin, and Hitler.

'Listen to this,' Martyn continued, reading from a wrinkled piece of paper. He was paraphrasing a well-known quote made before perhaps three thousand sannyasins one morning. 'Jews are always in search of their Adolph Hitlers, somebody who can kill them—then they feel at ease. When nobody bothers about them, then they are uneasy, the guilt follows . . . They create their Hitlers, and when I say this to you, you also remember: whenever you feel guilty, you create the punisher. You seek for punishment, because the punishment will make you guilt free . . . Don't feel guilty, otherwise you will seek punishment.'[2]

Rajneesh, in evolving a 'psychology of the Buddhas', was pressing the experiment of mind-blasting to the limits. Sensitive taboos were being surfaced and disgorged before a crowd of highly reactive human elements, and it could feed in a chain-reactive way.

'A Master is utterly destructive; a Master creates chaos. He

102

drives you insane as far as your mind is concerned—because when the mind has been driven insane, it stops . . . and suddenly a new consciousness arises.'[3]

Gurdjieff, the occult mystic, had elaborated on this teaching in an earlier era. But the armchair approach of today's Western dilettantes was just playing around. Rajneesh had true intent.

Martyn had told me that the German actress Eva Renzi was beaten and assaulted in August 1978 when she attended one of Rajneesh's supreme laboratories of mind-alteration, his encounter-group workshop. She fled the ashram bleeding. We would learn more about these encounter groups later. The real detective work was isolating, from Rajneesh's 30 million words printed in 350 books, the true points he was trying to make. Much of what he said was camouflage for the hooks which lay far deeper. My hunch was that the void-force in him had to be very careful in its surgery on this willing mob. Now and then a disclosure would leak out. I trusted my background and intuition in this domain to find his leaks. And there were leaks.

Regarding his experiments, Rajneesh had told a small group in Bombay (15 June 1970),

'So there are thousands of things on thousands of levels . . . Now all that I am saying is such that it can be talked about openly, but there are many things that cannot be openly disclosed and I shall not talk about them in public. I will talk about these matters only to those alone whom I think to be qualified for it . . . Even now, everything that I tell to persons cannot be disclosed publicly. Perhaps after another 2,500 years, it will be safe to tell certain things openly—that is, if man progresses in the area of spirituality.'[4]

The secret initiation was the goal. And there was a long line of eager sannyasins waiting for the boon, whatever it turned out to be. Until each sannyasin was ready, he would have to walk through a very complex maze of teachings and experiences, embracing what Judeo-Christianity, in its archaic lexicon, would term good and evil. Rajneesh conditioned them for an obstacle course of risks. It was akin to the gang of friends in his youth who broke the experience barriers by jumping off a high railroad bridge into a river. It was also reminiscent of the sayings of a man now in a California prison whose gang meat-axed Sharon Tate, wife of occult-movie producer Roman Polanski. I was on the way to India in 1969 when it happened. No one at the time had any category to place the statement of one of Manson's girls, Susan Atkins, who said,

'You really have to have a lot of love in your heart to do what I did to Tate.'[5]

America scratched its head over this one.

Rajneesh said to his sannyasins waiting in line,

'The mind says, "First know, then go into it. Without knowing, jumping into it is dangerous. You may be lost, or you may not come back again. Or, who knows whether this is good or bad? Divine or devil—who knows? So first know everything about it." But there is no way to know anything about it without going into it. That is the danger, that is the risk, the gamble. That's why I call sannyasins, "the gamblers". They are ready to go with me, without any hitch or hesitation, into the unknown. I cannot give them any guarantee . . . One has to take the risk; the danger is there. Either you will become enlightened or you will go mad— that danger is there . . . That's why a Master is needed . . . If you don't trust him, then madness is going to happen.'[6]

I was reading this from one of my magazines in the stack. Martyn and Ada were shaking their heads. Martyn had seen the same mentality in terrorist gangs in Europe. It was a mentality of anarchy. It blew the roof off of morality and could permit literally anything.

Such too was the consciousness-expansion of the ancient Tantrics of North India. It was the ritual that broke the taboo of conscience, that in turn wrought a deep change in the initiate. A kind of possession took place as the initiate was removed from his own humanity, his own society. And it was rumored that Rajneesh's deepest, most-cloaked experiments were of this Tantric variety. He spoke on Tantra all the time, and allowed people in his groups to participate in the popularized goodies. After all, many of them were frustrated medium-level management types whose lives in Europe and America had become sterile. What did they anticipate finding here with bubbling glee? The group orgies, of course. And they got them. Orgies, rapes, broken arms . . . and disappearances. In Tantra, you break every taboo. Every taboo. Conscience, that which divides the cosmos into good and evil, is the supreme enemy. What the mind calls evil must . . . must be embraced passionately. But depending on the level of the adept you are conditioning as Master, only so much can be divulged at a time.

Martyn and Ada followed me intently as I read the next morsel. Mind-destruction through meditation was the subject.

'You sit and just look . . . a thought of murdering somebody comes. Your mind is enjoying the thought of murdering somebody; this is one part. Another part of the mind says, "This is very bad, this is a sin . . ." You say, "This is my conscience." It is not your conscience; it has been put into you. It is the society controlling you from within; it is the strategy of the society to control you. You don't know what is right and what is wrong . . . Remember the ego wants to be identified with the good part, the moral part. It feels beautiful . . . You are just caught up by another part of the mind, you are still a slave. Your sinners and your saints, both are slaves. The real free man is free from both good and bad. He is beyond good and evil. He is just consciousness and nothing else.'[7]

Congressman Ryan was killed by Jim Jones's group in Guyana through the same teaching. Now the daughter of the dead congressman was a sannyasin. Irony within ironies. She would divulge to a reporter,

'I've heard other people say if Bhagavan asked them to kill themselves, they would do it. If Bhagavan asked them to kill someone else, they would do it. I don't know if my trust in him is that total. I would like it to be, and I don't believe he would ever do that.'[8]

Martyn was telling me of a similar statement made by one of the German sannyasins. Only certain people learned from history.

I concluded,

'As a child I used to stand amazed as I watched my grandfather trudge around his fenced-in chicken yard while they clucked at his feet. They would squawk like mad when he grabbed one, put its neck on a stump, and axed the head off to land into a squirting pool of blood. For ten or twenty seconds they would remember the event and flee him as he paced around the yard with the axe looking for the next chicken. Then they would slow, and hover

105

near his feet again. In under a minute he would pick another one up, put its head on the stump and axe it off.'

Martyn and Ada nodded their heads. We paid our bill, and wandered soberly into the Poona night air not far behind two more sannyasins in red . . . wandering off to the Rajneesh chicken yard.

15

AN ANARCHY OF MIND

Rajneesh Chandra Mohan was born on 11 December 1931 in the village of Kuchwada, in central India, a small farming village in the valley of the Vindhya mountains of Madhya Pradesh. He was the eldest son of a family with five sisters and six brothers. It is said that the child neither cried nor accepted any nourishment for the first three days. Rajneesh claims that this completed a fast he had begun 700 years before in another life, poised on the verge of enlightenment, which ended in his being murdered three days before the end of the twenty-one day fast. This was the classic fast of enlightenment, and according to Rajneesh, the final three days of the original fast were thus satisfied, thus making the fast overlap seven centuries from death to rebirth.

Rajneesh was born in the home of his maternal grandparents. His grandfather insisted on keeping the child with them due to financial difficulties that Rajneesh's father, Dadda, was having as a cloth merchant. Soon the maternal grandfather consulted a well-known Hindu astrologer who found the portent of Rajneesh both strange and ominous. The signs moved the astrologer to say,

'If this child survives after seven years, only then will I make the complete chart because it seems impossible that he can survive beyond seven years of age.'

From then on his whole family was troubled about the possibility that he might die.

Rajneesh, meanwhile, was brought up for his first seven years in the atmosphere of abundance that his maternal grandparents, relatively well-to-do people, were able to provide. Then at the seven-year mark, his grandfather, whom he was so attached to, died. As of that point, his fixation with death became a morbid passion, an obsession. Retrospectively Rajneesh comments,

'Death stared at me before the thrust of life began. For me the possibility of anyone else becoming my center was destroyed in the very first steps of my life.'[1]

A dehumanizing process began; the old mold fell away as a new image began to emerge. Rajneesh describes his facility of freedom from intimacy to be one's self totally, to be alone.

'Aloneness became my nature. (His grandfather's death) became for me the death of all attachments. Thereafter I could not establish a bond of relationship with anyone . . . From that day onward, every day, every moment, the awareness of life invariably became associated with the awareness of death.'[2]

His consequent move to his own family in a local village at the age of seven had its own trials. Rajneesh felt that through the death of his grandfather, he did in a sense go through a first death at the end of those seven years. His astrological chart now portrayed an impossible situation: that Rajneesh was to die every seven years until the age of twenty-one, when the 'death' would be irreversible. And indeed, that was to be when final 'Explosion' would occur.

Meanwhile, at seven, his first creative aptitude was to devise new ways of playing hookey from school. School he found to be meaningless, and there was not a single authority figure he could bring himself to respect.

'Everyone I found was very much involved in and with life. No one who had not seen death could ever become my teacher. I wanted to respect (them) but I could not. I could respect rivers, mountains, and even stones but not human beings.'[3]

Thus Rajneesh was thrown back upon himself as the final authority. And so he began to be viewed as a seditious rebel. And indeed new and more creative forms of perversity began to unfold in this unorthodox quest for meaning. As he says,

'I have never been initiated as a member of society—I have remained an individual, aloof.'[4]

So the orthodox rules, even at this age, had to go. He did his own thing—slept late, continued playing hookey, became an adept at practical jokes and broke up his school classes with uproarious debate and objections.

'People thought I was egotistical because I was not able to respect and honor anyone or obey anyone's command. Everyone felt I was an immodest and seditious rebel. And they had no hope that I would ever be any use to anyone.'[5]

What people believed in, he could not believe in. Customs and manners he ignored, from the standard *pranam* to the most elementary courtesy.

'If I had no trust, it was so. I could not help it. I never believed or felt that the truth could be learned from others. I knew there was only one way to learn, to learn from myself alone.'[6]

His first followers were members of his gang who he influenced into various 'dangerous exploits and outlandish mischief which put us in a collision course with society.'[7]

Life became an experiment in consciousness, breaking one mold after another. In the town of his youth, Gadarwara, there is a river called Shakkar (meaning 'sugar') which became a refuge and a point of focus for his experiments. He would play hookey there, bathe in the river, escape the people. He learned to swim one day by being thrown in three times in a row by his teacher. He responded to this vein of spontaneous, irrational, even brutal teaching. Rather than drown, he did learn to swim. Now here was a teacher, a swimming 'Master', he could relate to. One who tells him, 'There is no way to learn how to swim. I can just throw you in the water and then swimming comes of its own accord. There is no way to learn it—it cannot be taught. It is a knack, not knowledge.'[8] This made sense to Rajneesh.

The YMCA method of teaching swimming on the other hand would doubtless have been a stumbling-block, had its services been available. Rather this teacher merely stood looking down at the thrashing, drowning youth. Finally the random propeller motion of his hands became a lesson in total abandon. Rajneesh, touching noses with death, emerged wiser and now able to swim. The river continued being a refuge. On the river's edge, pretending to be out at the movies at night, Rajneesh would spend the evening lying naked in the sand of the river bank. Perhaps an experiment in total being.

As he approached the end of his second seven-year allotment of life, his experiments with death intensified. He fully expected to die. At times he involved friends and gang members in these experiments. One former member from that era observes,

'He would take us in the middle of a dark night on a walk along the river. He would then invite us to climb upon the high hills and

109

walk on the cliffs—it was a hair-raising experience. We were scared to death. Hundreds of feet below was the deep valley—one slip and we could have gone crashing down into pieces.'[9]

Other experiments involved rowing his gang members out into the river, tossing the non-swimmers in and then dunking them for maximum time. The question would follow, 'How was it?' He was driving himself and them towards experiences of total intensity.

Rajneesh's rule to his gang was 'try something new every day'. One biographer reports,

'Every day he did something new and different. He experimented with sleep by arranging unusual hours for rising and going to bed; he tried fasting, eating at strange hours; he meditated standing in the river, in the woods, under the falling rain. He experimented with the occult and yogic breath control, with magic and telekinesis.'[10]

Purportedly he would move coins on the library table at school by mental control.

The experiments continued. There was a high bridge over the river where people committed suicide. Here was a real opportunity for gang mind-expansion. The object? To play a form of blind man's bluff so that the mind short-circuits. And it did, as the air whistled by on the way down. As Rajneesh describes it:

'The bridge was very high to jump from . . . and before you reached the river there was a time in the gap between the bridge and the river when the mind would suddenly stop . . . I started inquiring how these moments can be made available without going to the mountains, to the river, to the bridges; how one can allow oneself to move into these spaces . . .'[11]

To do the bridge experiment they had to bribe a policeman to look the other way. It was a railway bridge, high up and off-limits.

Some of Rajneesh's experiments he had to do solo. As he approached the 'time of death' that the astrologers had earmarked, his face-to-face meetings with death reached an even more urgent abandon. Family and relatives would speak of these moments: Rajneesh would dive alone into a roaring monsoon-flooded river with rushing gorges and pockets of whirling water. He would scale a seventy-foot-high bridge and jump from there into the flooding river to be swept off.

'One of the most beautiful experiences,' according to Rajneesh, was jumping into the violent whirlpools where he would be sucked down to the bottom of the river. He learned to fight the natural tendency for survival and surrender on down through the current to the river's bottom. He was pressed to see the experience through to the end as 'the water moves round and round like a screw.'[12]

Finally the second predicted time of death had come, and Rajneesh felt ready to meet it head on. He went to the school principal, who by then was somewhat intimidated by the young rebel and his gang, and requested a seven-day leave of absence.

'I am going to retreat for seven days to wait for death. If it comes it is good to meet it consciously so that it becomes an experience.'

He got permission from an astounded principal. But everyone knew that Rajneesh had done more than enough homework. For as well as dangerous exploits, he had another unusual hobby, hanging around the cremation grounds.

'It was his common practice,' says one biographer, 'to follow people carrying a dead body to the cremation ground.'[13]

When his parents asked why he went to the cremation ground so often, to funerals of strangers, he told them,

'The man is not my concern. Death—it is such a beautiful phenomenon . . . One should not miss it.'[14]

And he rarely did—a figure in the background, huddled, as the flames consumed another body, sparks leaping into the night sky, Rajneesh would view death.

His seven-day leave of absence to die was spent at an old isolated temple in ruins near his village. He literally lay there in expectation of death, watching the process, as flies crawled across his face, and at one point a cobra crawled over him. He became a spectator of the process.

When he did not die, his phase of experiments continued on its prior course. Though he claimed that a part of him did die then. He had learned a deeper secret of abandon.

Back in the real world once again he continued to read voraciously and do the unusual. He marched to the beat of a different drummer. He rarely attended school, and became first a militant socialist, then a communist, and then he bounced from cause to cause, letting each one run its course. He may have even qualified as India's first hippie, growing his hair down to his shoulders. When his dad told him to cut it off, he went the extra mile and shaved his skull (a sign of the death of one's father in India), hence further conditioning his father that he could in no way impose his paternal will on his son. He was transcending social conditioning:

'Once you are caught in it you become incapable of thinking, seeing.'[15]

Rajneesh continued to evolve different pranks, all geared at what he termed 'the right victim': coins glued to pavements, people told gruesome tales so that their superstitions would be exaggerated. Then there was the treatment of the local doctor. Rajneesh's gang would stop and read the doctor's sign board with all his impressive degrees. Stentorian announcements would flood the streets. It became a solemn ritual. In the end the sign was removed. All local egos were levelled. For they had in their midst a great sage. Yet through it all Rajneesh opened up to no one and was vulnerable to no one. Says Vasant Joshi,

'In experiencing his aloneness, Rajneesh became more of an outsider, a stranger. He became rooted in a state of detachment in which even in the midst of activities and people, he remained unidentified, an outsider.'

As Rajneesh puts it so eloquently,

'I became a universe unto myself.'[16]

He graduated from the village high school in 1951 and at nineteen went on to a local college, Hitkarini College, where he lasted a year. Out on his ear, he then wheeled and dealed with the principal to get him into another college. The Jain College at Jabalpur took the gamble. Soon it became evident that he was such a disruption in class that they had to bend the rules— Rajneesh gets his way again—and not require him to attend lectures. He would appear for exams, otherwise he went to work with a local paper at an editorial job that he briefly held on to. His search became acutely solitary and he 'almost went mad'.[17] He accepted no authority apart from direct experience.

Rajneesh describes this intermediate college era:

'Throughout the night and day . . . questions hovered around me . . . I was in a deep sea, so to speak, without any boat or bank anywhere. Whatever boats had been there, I had myself sunk or denied.'[18]

Rajneesh felt it was better to drown than step on to another's boat. There was a spiritual momentum going on deep within.

'My condition was one of utter darkness. It was as if I had fallen into a deep, dark well. In those days I had many times dreamt that I was falling and falling and going deeper into a bottomless well.

'And many times I . . . awakened from a dream full of perspiration, sweating profusely, because the falling was endless without any ground or place to rest my feet . . . for me there was no clear path. It was all darkness. Every next step for me was in darkness—aimless and ambiguous. My condition was full of tension, insecurity, and danger.'[19]

He was caught, committed, and hooked to this one-way path, down the tube without bending his ear to an outside guide. He was sealed on his own road built to his own terms. He would go berserk should courage or patience slip him for a second.

This intensely dark phase lasted a year. He was rapidly approaching the age of twenty-one, the predicted certain year of death. He was being sucked into the whirlpool. He describes it himself:

'For one year it was almost impossible to know what was happening . . . Just to keep myself alive was a very difficult thing, because all appetite disappeared. Days would pass and I would not feel any hunger . . . I had to force myself to eat and drink. The body was so non-existential that I had to hurt myself to feel that I was still in the body. I had to knock my head against the wall to feel whether my head was still there or not. Only when it hurt would I be a little in my body.

'Every morning and every evening I would run five to eight miles. People used to think that I was mad. It was just to feel myself . . . not lose contact. I could not talk to anybody because everything had become so inconsistent that even to formulate one sentence was difficult. In the middle of a sentence I would forget what I was saying; in the middle of the way I would forget where I was going. Then I would have to come back.

'I had to keep myself shut up in my room. I made it a point not

113

to talk, not to say anything, because to say anything was to say I was mad. For one year this persisted. I would simply lie on the floor and look at the ceiling and count from one to a hundred and then back from a hundred down to one again. Just to remain capable of counting was at least something. Again and again I would forget. It took one year for me to gain a focus again, to have a perspective.'[20]

During all of this, massive headaches came and went and his two cousins with whom he was living became very worried.

16

THE FINAL DISAPPEARING ACT

The spiritual and psychological terrain that Rajneesh now had to enter was so alien, so dehumanizing, so against all inbuilt mechanisms of human survival, conscience, will and intuition, that it took a total act of abandon to cross the chasm. Herein lies a mystery. The average person would have bailed out eons ago. It takes a certain cosmic desperation, almost suicidal drive, to go this route. In a sense a man has to feel an irreversible abhorrence towards life and the world, to regard anything alien as better. One also has to take very seriously the belief that one is in fact God. And in these matters Rajneesh excelled. The ordinary existence was not even an option. He would overturn that plate without so much as looking at it. It was become God or nothing (or both).

'Now it was beyond me, it was happening. I had done something unknowingly, I had knocked at the door. Now the door had opened. I had been meditating for many years, just sitting silent doing nothing . . . a presence, a watcher.'[1]

The intensity of Rajneesh's meditations mounted and mounted, in this huge thrust. The Final Explosion was in sight, around any corner it sat unexpected.

One powerful setting for meditation was at the top of a tree where Rajneesh would sit, a method he had been using for years. A year prior to Explosion the tree meditations followed classic occult guidelines:

'I used to climb up a tall tree and get myself engrossed in meditation for hours every night. One night I got so lost in meditation that I did not know when my body fell down from the tree. I looked about askance when I saw my body lying on the ground . . . It was a very queer experience. A bright line, a glittering silver cord from the naval of my body was joined on to me up above where I was perched on the tree . . . That day was the first time I saw my own body from outside, and since that day the mere physical existence of my body finished forever . . . That was the most important moment: my realization of the spirit that is within every human body.'[2] (He had been a militant atheist for years driven to seek answers solely by experiences.)

As morning dawned, two village women carrying milk cans saw the body while the 'spirit' of Rajneesh in the tree was observing. Finally one of the women came over and touched his forehead and he blipped back in again, reviving before them on the ground. But later he would ponder the Tantric implications of this experience—the yoga of sexual enlightenment. Reflecting on what happened after reviving on the ground he added,

'Many more experiences of this sort happened to me and I understood why in India those spiritualists who carried on experiments in *samadhi* (mindless enlightenment) and the fact of death got women to collaborate with them.[3]

'Thereafter I experienced this phenomenon six times within the period of six months. During those eventful six months, I felt that my life-span became less by ten years: that is to say, if I was to live seventy years, now with these experiences I would only live a life of sixty years. Such extraordinary experiences I had in those six months. The hair on my chest turned white and I failed to grasp the meaning of all these happenings.'[4]

Rajneesh would recall that during this period there was an infinite emptiness, a hollowness emerging. There was no doer. He lost the usual ambitions, even, he claims, the desire for enlightenment which he called 'the Buddha disease'. As Explosion inched closer, Rajneesh observes,

'One day a questionless condition came about. It is not that I received The Answer—no. Rather all questions just fell away and a great void was created. This was an explosive situation. Living in that condition was as good as dying. And then the person died who had been asking the questions. After that experience of void, I asked no questions.'[5]

This indeed was quite a contrast. After all, it was his endless questions, his frenetic dissatisfaction with any answers that drove him and drove him and alienated him in class after class in school.

The reason he was thrown out of his first college was the endless barrage of questions and objections he would raise in class. So a significant personality change was appearing.

The final week before the Explosion took place, the tidal waves of radical consciousness rolled in, inundating Rajneesh with the truly extraordinary. A new energy surrounded him, arising out of nowhere. The description of the Explosion would be articulated in full by the subject of the experience, Rajneesh himself, who would recount it to his ardent devotees sitting at his feet twenty years later, and ready to hear it. It would occur exactly seven years after the 'death' experience he went through at the old temple at fourteen. Now he was twenty-one, the fated age when the astrologers said a final death would occur. There was no way that they could see how he could live through it. The date of Explosion was 21 March 1953—an irreversible event.

'Seven days I lived in a very hopeless and helpless state, but at the same time something was arising. When I say hopeless I don't mean what you mean by the word hopeless. I simply mean there was no hope in me. Hope was absent . . . The hopelessness was absolute and total. Hope had disappeared and with it its counterpart, hopelessness, had also disappeared. It was a totally new experience—of being without hope. It was not a negative state . . . it was absolutely positive. It was not just absence, a Presence was felt. Something was overflowing in me, over-flooding me. And when I saw I was helpless, I don't mean the word in the dictionary sense. I simply say I was selfless . . . I have realized the fact that I am not, so I cannot depend on myself, so I cannot stand on my own ground . . . I was in . . . a bottomless abyss . . . There was no fear because there was nobody to be afraid.

'Those seven days were of tremendous transformation, total transformation. And the last day the presence of a totally new energy, a new light . . . became so intense that it was almost unbearable, as if I was exploding, as if I was going mad with blissfulness . . . It was impossible to make any sense out of . . . what was happening. It was a very non-sense world—difficult to figure out, difficult to manage in categories . . . It was like a tidal wave of bliss.

'The whole day was strange . . . and it was a shattering experience. The past was disappearing, as if it had never belonged to me, as if I had read about it somewhere, as if I had dreamed about it, as if it was somebody else's story I have heard and somebody told it to me. I was becoming loose from my past, I was being uprooted from my history, I was losing my autobiography. I was becoming a non-being, what Buddha calls *Anatta*. Boundaries were disappearing, distinctions were disappearing.

'Mind was disappearing; it was millions of miles away. It was difficult to catch hold of it, it was rushing farther and farther away, and there was no urge to keep it close . . . By the evening it became so difficult to bear it—it was hurting, it was painful. It was like when a woman goes into labor when a child is born, and the woman suffers tremendous pain—the birth pangs.

'I used to go to sleep on those days about twelve or one in the night, but that day it was impossible to remain awake. My eyes were closing, it was difficult to keep them open. Something was very imminent, something was going to happen . . . something like death, something very drastic, something that will be either death or a new birth, a crucifixion or a resurrection—but something of tremendous import was just around the corner. And it was impossible to keep my eyes open . . . Asleep and awake together, the whole body relaxed, every cell of the body totally relaxed . . . and yet a light of awareness burns within you . . . clear, smokeless . . . The body is in the deepest sleep possible and your consciousness is at its peak . . .

'It was weird. For the first time it shocks you to the very roots, it shakes your foundations. You can never be the same after that experience . . . Near about twelve my eyes suddenly opened—I had not opened them. The sleep was broken by something else. I felt a great presence around me in the room. It was a very small room. I felt a throbbing life all around me, a great vibration— almost like a hurricane, a great storm of light . . . I was drowning in it.

'It was so tremendously real that everything became unreal. The walls of the room became unreal, the house became unreal, my own body became unreal . . .

'That night another reality opened its door, another dimension became available. Suddenly it was all there, the other reality, the separate reality, the really Real, or whatsoever you want to call it—call it God, call it Truth, call it Dharmma, call it Tao, or

118

whatsoever you will. It was nameless. But it was there—so opaque, so transparent, and yet so solid one could have touched it. It was almost suffocating me in that room. It was too much and I was not yet capable of absorbing it.

'A deep urge arose in me to rush out of the room, to go under the sky—it was suffocating me. It was too much. IT WILL KILL ME! If I had remained a few moments more, it would have suffocated me—it looked like that.

'I rushed out of the room, came out into the street. A great urge was there just to be under the sky with the stars, with the trees, with the earth . . . to be with nature. And immediately as I came out, the feeling of being suffocated disappeared. It was too small a place for that big phenomenon. Even the sky is a small place for that big phenomenon . . . It is bigger than the sky. Even the sky is not the limit for it.

'I was walking towards the nearest garden. It was a totally new walk, as if gravitation had disappeared. I was walking, or I was running, or I was simply flying; it was difficult to decide. There was no gravitation, I was feeling weightless—as if some energy was taking me. I was in the hands of some other energy.

'For the first time I was not alone, for the first time I was no more an individual, for the first time the drop had come and fallen into the ocean. Now the whole ocean was mine, I was the ocean. There was no limitation. A tremendous power arose as if I could do anything whatsoever. I was not there, only the power was there . . . The gardeners were fast asleep. I had to enter the garden like a thief, I had to climb the gate. But something was pulling me towards the garden. It was not within my capacity to prevent myself. I was just floating.

'That's what I mean when I say again and again, "float with the river, don't push the river." . . . I was not there, IT was there, call IT God—God was there. I would like to call it IT, because God is too much of a word and has become dirty through too much use, so let me call it IT. IT was there and I was just carried away, carried by a tidal wave.

'The moment I entered the garden everything became luminous. IT was all over the place—the benediction, the blessedness . . . One tree was tremendously luminous, the maulshree tree. It attracted me, it pulled me toward itself. I had not chosen it. God

119

himself had chosen it. I went to the tree; I sat under the tree. As I sat there things started settling. The whole universe became a benediction.

'It is difficult to say how long I was in that state . . . But it was infinity. It had nothing to do with clock time; it was timeless. Those three hours became the whole eternity, endless eternity. There was no time, there was no passage of time. It was the virgin reality—uncorrupted, untouchable, immeasurable. And that night, something happened that has continued . . . Each moment it has been happening again and again. It has been a miracle, each moment.'[6]

Rajneesh discloses an element of the miraculous:

'That night and since that night, I have never been in the body. I am hovering around it. I became tremendously powerful and, at the same time, very fragile. I became very strong, but that strength is not the strength of a rock, that strength is the strength of a rose flower . . . But I have never been in the body again. I am just hovering around the body. And that's why I say it has been a tremendous miracle. Each moment I am surprised: I am still here? I should not be. I should have left any moment, but still I am here. Every morning I open my eyes and I say, "So, again I am still here?"—because it seems almost impossible.'[7]

17

THE EMERGING VEDIC SUPERMAN

Those who have seen the film *Invasion of the Body Snatchers*, have an analogy by which to view the Rajneesh transformation. On one day, and up until then, the person next door was an ordinary person. The next day the body looked virtually the same, except for maybe a few of the mannerisms up close. But suddenly something totally alien has taken residence inside the body and it is now completely disguised. The gulf between how it looks on the outside and what dwells on the inside could not be greater. The new resident has been floating across the galaxies for thousands of years, through unthinkable regions, and its origins go back to a totally alien civilization in a far removed planetary system with totally different laws and thoughts. The original resident has been extinguished, dissolved, digested.

Rajneesh describes it,

'In that explosion, the old man of yesteryear died. This new man is absolutely new. The man who was walking on the path is dead and is no more. What is, is a new man altogether . . . There is no story after that explosion; there are no events after it. All events are before the explosion. After the explosion there is only void. Whatever was before is not me or mine.'[1]

He elaborates a little more at another time, disclosing a mystery:

'I became non-existential and became existence. That night I died and was reborn. But the one that was reborn has nothing to do with that which died, it is a discontinuous thing . . . The one who died died totally; nothing of him has remained . . . not even a shadow. It died totally, utterly . . . That day of March twenty-first, the person who had lived for many, many lives, for millennia, simply died. Another being, absolutely new, not connected at all with the old, started to exist.'[2]

'I have known many other deaths, but they were nothing compared to it; they were partial deaths. Sometimes the body died, sometimes a part of the mind died, sometimes a part of the ego died, but as far as the person was concerned, it remained . . . That night the death was total. It was a date with death and God simultaneously.'[3]

The body in whom the new consciousness resided continued the momentum of the prior existence, going to school, eating and what not. But relatives make no dispute over the fact that there was a new resident. Rajneesh the Non-Being, graduated from College, went on to get an M.A., and then took up a teaching job at the College of Jabalpur, from where he first graduated. The new consciousness evolved its tactics and techniques over this twelve-year period of professorship. Rajneesh spent four days travelling across India for every day he spent at Jabalpur.

He was gaining notoriety, momentum, opposition, and end-less controversial press coverage. He severed completely with the college in the later half of the 1960s and became a wandering guru. It was not until 1969 that he actually initiated his first disciples, bringing together the outward structure of what has become his practice of today—giving people a new name, a *mala* with his picture on it, and so on. In 1970, he moved to Bombay to live and watch his following expand and expand. Westerners spread the word, and the following exploded geometrically.

Then in 1974, Rajneesh moved to Poona, the great Indian center of his activities. Poona, as we have seen, is a wealthy city by Indian standards, and its weather is among some of the most bearable in India. It would be ideal for his experiments in con-sciousness, and it would tolerate some of the unbelievable things he would do. He would have the local government officialdom in his back pocket, he would get no strong opposition from the staunchly Hindu population, and land and buildings he would get galore. By the mid-1970s he would enter the big league of the Super-Gurus with all the celebrity trappings of air-conditioned Mercedes Benzes, visiting princes and movie stars, and un-dreamed-of wealth—wealth that the meager, rural, younger Rajneesh would not have thought possible. It seemed that he had entered a special slot in the fast flow of history. He had dived into the roaring currents of history's waterfall, and the world of events was in his, Its, the Non-Being's hands.

The towering forces and events that went together to create this creature, the Rajneesh Non-Being, had a will, a purpose, and a plan in history. In part it was to replicate It's own consciousness and form a 'New Man' from among the ranks of willing mortals who would lay down their lives, their existences, as living sacrifices, and the willing playthings of this colossal Being, or Non-Being. It is in this context that the magic happens, the miracle of transmogrification.

Now someone who was the man or woman next door in Sweden, Germany, or America, suddenly becomes the fully unrecognizable 'Other'. Such would be the role of the initiate, the 'sannyasin', who in the hands of his master, Rajneesh, would be a subject in the experimental laboratory until he became the new creature of his Master and turned into the 'New Man' in this alchemist's hands. It is only in this context that Rajneesh's consciousness-engineering can be understood and why some of the incredible things go on that go on in his experiments in creating the 'New Man'. Like a spider weaving a vast web, he has created a formidable structure. Only when one is on the inside and knows the rules, does it make sense in a bizarre and frightening way, as we shall see.

18

ZORBA THE BUDDHA CAFE

It was several days later at the ashram. We were at the outdoor cafe and pavilion on another part of the ashram, which still required walking past a gate guard and sentry box. This oasis of leisure had a copacabana bar, with an awning and terrace, that served exotic mixed drinks. It was reminiscent of Old Town San Diego. They also served sandwiches. Grafted to that was a New Age vegetarian restaurant with carrot breads, whole-grain and half-grain breads and cakes, yogurt concoctions, exotic Indian fruit cups, ice creams—all items that Westerners of the California vintage fantasize about when they are on Indian trains.

I met up with Martyn and Ada and their daughter Michelle. The cafe was our checkpoint as we wandered here and there talking to people, if we were not relaxing at our large circular table.

For most of the time that Martyn and I were probing Rajneesh's realm, Ada and Michelle stayed in the diesel truck parked in the cool shade in a nearby park. It had a kitchen and the back end would open up into a kind of sun porch, so she and Michelle could sit in the living-room section of the truck, sip herbal tea and watch the red tide stroll by. Now and then people would come up and talk. Ada was from Amsterdam and had been in India for years. She was *sympathique* and attuned to what they were saying, so she was a ready audience. She had been on the guru trail herself, with Martyn, so few of the ideas were new. Michelle was only three, and so would run around Indian style, half-dressed, like a lot of the ashram children. At the cafe, they blended right in.

Martyn had been over at a table talking to a girl. Now he was consoling her as she was crying. He had his arm around her, reassuring her. None of this was new to Ada. They had both dealt with a lot of people. The place gave her the creeps, but she pretended it didn't. She had tea and a coffee cake. I had coffee with cardamon pods and a brownie. Michelle was face deep in chocolate ice-cream.

I gathered that the girl confiding in Martyn was in tears over the fact that she was now sterilized—at twenty-six—and was running out of money. Usually she could operate in the 'blissed-out' mode, but now and then things like this would jar her field of awareness. Perhaps Michelle reminded her of what she could never have—children. Martyn and the attractive sannyasin girl were at a nearby table in a corner. Ada and I were reflecting together about various things as I went through the stack of magazines. Ada whispered to me across the table the substance of the problem. She was within earshot. Ada whispered,

'I cannot imagine what it would be like to have twenty, thirty intense relationships with different guys in one year. And then do this year after year. After a while you would become . . . schizophrenic. You would be an old wasted dog by the time you were thirty-five and then nobody would touch you. You would be thrown away, discarded, used up.'

Some of the older women did look deeply troubled. I had seen a number of faces creased with grief—fading flowers, fading fast. It reminded me of the Eloi in H.G. Wells' *The Time Machine*, adult-children living by the pleasure principle, without depth, without ability to think beyond the now, completely dependent on the system to succor them, and rendered absolutely incapable of dealing with what we call 'the world'.

'Listen to this,' I announced as Ada's ears perked up. She leaned forward on the table. Ada and I had been discussing Rajneesh's abolition of the family and what role that played in his creation of the 'New Man', in his communal experiment, 'The Buddhafield'.

'Man has outgrown the family. The utility of the family is finished . . . it has been very harmful because it has corrupted the human mind. But there was no alternative in the past, there was no way to choose anything else. It was a necessary evil . . . A few people may still choose to have a family . . . It will be a very small percentage . . . But for the greater majority, the family is an ugly thing. You can ask the psychoanalysts and they will say all kinds of mental diseases arise out of the family. All kinds of psychosis, neurosis, arise out of the family. The family creates a very, very ill human being.'

Ada had seen some pretty ill human beings in our midst. I went on,

'In a commune a child will have a richer soul. He will know many women, he will know many men, he will not be addicted to one person or two persons . . . And the children should be of all. They should not carry the badge of their family. They will belong to the commune, the commune will take care of them.'

Ada looked disgusted. We had both seen the ashram children, and they were a nightmare of studied anarchy.

'This will be the most revolutionary step in human history.'

I shared with Ada how the evening before, when Martyn and I had spent time here at the cafe, we passed three ashram girls as we left, aged about eight, nine, and ten, hanging around at the gate and slouching against the fence, taking controlled drags on their cigarettes like they had been doing it for years. One gave us a studied, sidelong glance of the Saint Tropez variety. Jaded. The experience of middle-age before life had even begun.

Rajneesh's teachings continued, making the permissive approach of Doctor Spock appear like the harsh intolerance of a Jesuit school.

'Now the very idea of bringing children up is nonsense . . . you cannot bring them up. The very idea of bringing children up is nonsense—not only nonsense, very harmful, immensely harmful . . . the moment you start creating patterns and characters around them, you are imprisoning them . . . Each generation goes on giving its neurosis to the new people that come to the earth. And the society persists, with all its madness and misery . . . If your husband is laughing with somebody else, it is good. Your husband is laughing—laughter is always good . . . Your woman is holding somebody else's hand—good. Warmth is flowing, the flow of warmth is good, it is a value. With whom it happens is immaterial.'[1]

The carousel approach.

'Yeah, till you are an old rag and nobody wants to touch you,' Ada interjected.

When a married couple (Mira and Shiva) approached Rajneesh after an encounter group, he told them,

'It's better to change partners than to destroy love, because love is the goal not the partner. If love isn't happening with one person, then let it happen with someone else . . . I call a relationship pathological when you're clinging only for clinging's sake . . . It loses all joy, loses all charm, loses all magnetism. It becomes ill, pathological . . . So if love is happening, then stay together. If it's not happening, then give each other the chance to find love with someone else.'

Rajneesh looked at the German sannyasin, Shiva, at that point and said, 'So, Shiva . . .?' And that ended the marriage.[2]

My eyes fell on the next quote silently. By now Ada was holding Michelle close, and bouncing her on her knee.

'Let the children see, play, enjoy. While their parents are making love, let them be there. Let them be a part of it, let them watch . . . what happens to the child's mother when she makes love. How ecstatic her face, how her eyes close and she goes deep into herself; how the father becomes orgasmic, how he screams with joy. Let the children know. Let the children know many people loving. They will become rich.'[3]

A few moments later, Martyn and Ada switched places at the girl's table, and I slid the last quote towards Martyn, who shook his head soberly.

Martyn recounted what Ada had overheard regarding the girl's despondency over her sterility. Rajneesh had dealt with an identical situation more than once. His answer?

'Many times sannyasins come to me, particularly women, and they say, "We want to have children." . . . When I look into them all that I see is that they are wanting to have revenge on their mothers. Whatsoever their mothers have done to them, they want children, so they can do it to them . . . What relief comes? It is a catharsis, a vomit. It is very rarely that out of love you think of a child . . . That is the only way you can take revenge on your mother; there is no other way.'[4]

The article does not say whether Rajneesh's answer satisfied the girl or her yearning for a child, or her despair over her permanent sterility.

On this part of the ashram, across the street from the main part where stood Rajneesh's residence, the Lao Tzu house, the ashram workers toiled long hours in the sun. These were the privileged permanent residents, who had given the ashram their entire savings and burned all their bridges to move in. Their days would consist of eleven hours a day and more of duty to Bhagavan. They would manicure the gardens, till the fields, build cabins, plant sunflowers and a range of crops, work in the woodshops, bakeries, printing press—like the elves of an enchanted kingdom. The luxury of the idle rich who did not have to work was not their inheritance. That was a more elite group on the ashram, those with a fortune. The marginally well-to-do and less had to work. And the first flavors of total freedom, which attracted them in a syrup of sensuality, in time would become a tight daily regime. In the steamy sun, their brains could contemplate the cryptic teachings of their godman whom they served night and day and worshipped. This was an outer skin on the body of the communal experiment. Now and then they would buckle under the pressure, fight, fall apart. But they were addicts of this kingdom for life, dependent upon this new society, and could never quite return to everyday life, life in the world.

These were the serfs, the medieval servants of the king, and in a caste role whether they knew it or not. We passed them, toiling sweaty bodies from all over the world—Brazilians, British, Germans, Canadians, Australians, Japanese, Swedes, and Indians. Sweaty and covered with dirt, sawdust, hay, or stubble on the wet matted hair of their naked chests. Heaving and groaning, screaming at each other or joking, the work went on.

Release they would get, because women outnumbered them three to one. And many of these girls, most of them, seemed picked out of the sky—it was uncanny. So many lithe, well-developed beauties, at the flower of life. Sensual, dark, beautied Italians and Jewesses, heavenly Scandinavians, sultry French women and Brazilians . . . handpicked, it seemed, by the gods, as though a magnet had pulled them from around the world. Yes, these heaving studs would have their release. And if swapping partners did not do the trick, there was Nepalese hash, or opium, or regular pot. There were also a range of encounter groups where they could release their rages and perversities. There was primal scream, and there was a padded cell where they could beat each other's brains out, and many of them did.

Martyn and I talked to two of them in the carpenter's shop and were greeted with acute suspicion. They would not talk, so we continued on our perusal of the premises. We heard swearing in every language known to man. Not all were content in this realm of the elves. And under a thorn bush somewhere, away from any listeners, I read in *Sannyas* magazine how Rajneesh had carved out, through the subtle craft of his words, a place in his kingdom for the merry elves, albeit not always functioning on the level of ecstasy.

Now and then, at the evening darshans, one of them would be given the boon of bringing the master a question. For instance, consider Rajneesh's response to a question from one of the merry elves of his realm:

'Just the other day Divyananda came to me—he works in my garden—and he said, "What is happening to me? I have become almost a Zombie, and I am afraid. Should I go and do something else?" And I told him, "You be a Zombie. Be a perfect Zombie, that's all. You continue your work." Now something immensely valuable is happening, but he cannot understand it yet. This is what is happening: catalepsy. He's open to me, and working in my garden. He has become even more open to me. He is in a shock, he is forgetting who he is. He is losing his old identity, he is paralyzed! Why paralyzed? Because the old cannot function and the new has yet to be born. So he is in the interval.'

According to Rajneesh we were in a garden of Zombies, sci-fi androids. And it was good for them. But there was more to this madness:

'This is going to happen to many. Don't be afraid when it happens . . . This is a state of not knowing; you don't know what is what, all your knowledge is lost, all your cleverness is gone. You become idiotic. You look like an idiot! People will say that you have become hypnotized or something, that you are no longer your old self. That is true; but it is a kind of shock. And good, because it will destroy the past . . . That is the whole meaning of sannyas and discipleship: that your past has been completely washed away—your memory, your ego, your identity—all has to go.'⁵

I surveyed the horizon at that point and concurred with Rajneesh. He was right, they indeed were zombies in the garden, as he would say, 'perfect zombies'. How much more clearly could he have said it? I was grateful that I was not one of them. Now and then there were accidents, the kind of accidents I guess Zombies have. Things like hands cut off on the old buzz saw . . . the buzz-saw enlightenment routine. Yes, we saw a lot of bandages. And we did catch an occasional scream now and then. Yet one might ask, were these wails of pain fruitless endeavors? By no means indeed! The Master had a plan. And here it is (to continue Rajneesh's discourse on Zombies),

'And each Master beheads you, cuts your head mercilessly, destroys your reason, destroys your logic, brings you down from the head. And the only way is to cut the head completely. This is the third state: catharsis. When the head is no longer functioning, its control is lost and the prisoner is set free . . . That's why a real disciple passes through a kind of insanity around a Master.'[6]

Rajneesh had named it, and now they were claiming it.

So we headed out of the gate, without passing 'go' or collecting two hundred, Ada dragging Michelle by the hand, next Martyn, and then myself—in that order to be sure. You could say we had had enough for the day . . . to be sure.

19

THE ORANGE LIZARD

The bamboo villages sit in a cluster along the river, which flows along the edges of Poona. The surrounding is pristine, primeval. The villages are a mile from the ashram, and are the habitation of long-term sannyasins not privy enough to live on the ashram.

Each abode is built by hand, fashioned out of bamboo, straw, and jute. They resemble wicker houses. Some are very chic. They come as huts, lofts, tree-houses. Some are almost full-fledged houses—two-storied with balconies, verandahs, hanging plants—very elaborate. I pass a very attractive dwelling. It is airy, open, without a lock. A mosquito net hangs over the wide arabesque door. Hanging plants surround a water-bed, a battery stereo sits nearby. On the walls are prints for the culturatti, maybe a Modigliani or a Gauguin. Center-stage sits a picture of Rajneesh, staring into the bed. A flute lies nearby. Through the tiny dwelling is a living-room view of the river flowing by. It is the model Eastern dream house. I pass on. From different huts come muffled groans and giggles, as men and women unashamedly go at it. Whiffs of aromatic smoke drift out into the air, the smell of Nepalese hashish. It is eleven in the morning. Then I see a microcosmic event.

Below in the miniature world of the rocks and foliage a drama ensues. I see one of those strange-looking, bright orange horned reptiles occasionally seen in India. Staring at it icily from behind is a black cat. The lizard freezes; only its neck moves as it breathes. Then the terror begins. The lizard scurries. The cat paces it by inches. It circles. A paw. It does a belly roll. The paw shows what it can do to the lizard's belly. It flips and runs. This time the cat has it in its mouth. It freezes. The cat slowly chews, lightly. The cat drops it. The lizard runs like mad, dashing between two rocks. The cat is right behind it, nose near the tail. It freezes in the crevice. A paw flips it out into the sunlight. It flutters insanely.

131

The yellow eyes close down on it. This goes on back and forth. Off it flutters. Every time it flutters off, there is some part of it missing. It is a studied process in dismemberment. In the background to this event are crescendos of groans issuing from this hut and that.

Now the lizard has been half engorged by the cat, its lower half hanging obscenely out. It looks like Chronos devouring his children. The orange body spews out in a half vomit. It flutters. This time the cat clamps down on the skull. There are loud pops and the fluttering ceases. The dead body is hurled onto a flat rock. I leave the village, contemplating the microcosmic event.

It is a time for evaluating untold numbers of images I have seen. It is also a time to admit that interlayered with the horrifying and obviously repulsive, cultish, and evil aspects so apparent here, these thousands of Westerners are not all pulled here for completely mad reasons. It is a difficult puzzle and these people are hard to write off, because there are so many seductive hooks that give them a reason to be here. There is something for everybody—the lonely, the disconsolate, the bored, the hedonistic, and those who have worked through all the pat answers to life. There is plenty to chew on for the intellectual. There is also sex, security, a kind of oozing love, adventure, and a deep sense of mission. For companionship, the Rajneesh toy-shed abounds with talented, interesting, attractive, sensual members of the opposite sex. It is a cornucopia that pulls the Westerners here for a thousand reasons. Those with middle-management burnout, those rejected by their families, recent divorcees, as well as the super-bright, avant-garde, and jet-set variety.

Terence Stamp has come to have a look, so has Diana Ross, and many have joined—Pat Lear, heiress of Lear Jets, McVicker, inventor of Play-doh, Richard Price, co-founder of Esalen, who has been given a new name by Rajneesh. On and on the list goes of the famous, fashionable, and well-to-do. They can't all be written off as a minority of unstable fanatics, casting their lives upon the sacrificial altar of some alien god. That is a comfortable pigeonhole that a threatened outsider uses to dismiss the true threat. But once on the inside—or once one is near the perimeter and vulnerable—the attractiveness of the lure into this kingdom

132

should not be taken lightly. True, what those lured into the kingdom ultimately encounter may be a million miles from what the road-signs told them. But all the same, the pull is considerable. One is forced to believe that some sort of seduction of considerable power is in effect, not to be shrugged off lightly.

Gifted Indian author Gita Mehta, writer of *Karma Cola*, saw the seductive effect:

'God sat in a cushioned swivel chair with a blue denim hat on his head and spoke about the revolution. As the discourse gathered momentum it became clear that God was an intellectual snob. He dropped only the heaviest names. Jesus, Marx, Mahavira. And Fritz Perls. His two-thousand-odd devotees inhaled, writhed, or listened in an ecstasy of being.'[1]

Rajneesh's personal library is one of the largest in the world—200,000 volumes. He is said to devour books at the prodigious rate of twenty books a day. Rajneesh was not a back-woods Indian guru like Muktananda who needed a Ram Dass. Rajneesh had no need for a Ram Dass. He could stun his savvy, up-beat audience with his own erudition and superconsciousness. He could be cute, cool, shocking, scintillating, perverse, and infinitely alien and infinitely unreachable.

Rajneesh would net in the culturatti like fine prawns with piquant observations like, 'But Sartre thinks freedom creates anguish, and freedom is a kind of condemnation, a curse. And Kierkegaard says, "Man is a constant trembling." And Buddha wants you to go into this freedom . . . Sariputra is ready now.'[2] Delightfully sage. Superconsciousness means superconsciousness. And this audience in the West has high expectations in its romantically-nurtured view of what superconsciousness is. Westerners don't like bad theater or awkward delivery. They don't like to make alibis, as when the Godman talks in baby talk, or mumbles. 'Omniscient?' they might ask, in faltering unbelief. But when the Godman can talk about Marcuse, Wittgenstein, A. J. Ayer, then Sylvia Plath, along with Advaita and the Upanishads . . . then he has arrived. They will listen. Throw in guru comments about existential despair, modern Dada art, and other avant-garde subjects and you have a formidable package.

Now add to our shelf of ingredients the lure of the esoteric that every New-Age Westerner is in search of, and cast that in a

Romantic light, with all the imagery to fire the mystical imagination, and the oracle becomes irresistible. Rajneesh knew how to inject the most colorful fantasies with hidden revelation, whether it concerned the neurology of the *kundalini*, the radiance of aura fields, or 'the externalization of the hierarchy', a prize New-Age subject. Consider the following delicacy:

Esoteric groups

Rajneesh confesses he has contact with the ascended masters, those exalted, non-physical superbeings inhabiting the higher planes. They are known as 'esoteric groups'. (Remember Ram Dass?) Rajneesh says,

'I have been in contact with many esoteric groups.'[3]

One day he divulges a secret. One of the heaviest groups of spirit powers are 'The Ashoka Nine'. They were the powers behind Adolph Hitler and Nazism. They were 'behind the whole thing. They were trying to capture the whole world . . . The whole East was inwardly with Hitler because the (esoteric) group that was working behind him was an Eastern group.'[4] But the ascended powers misfired. Rajneesh explains that even though they controlled Hitler's ego, it just got in the way and their effort to save humanity failed.

On another occasion he talks about a world spiritual explosion, another New-Age theme. The subject is the massive preparation that the Theosophical Movement undertook to prepare their Messiah, Krishnamurthi, to be the vehicle of Maitreya:

'Therefore the Theosophists selected four or five small children—because it could not be confidently predicted how each child will develop. They selected Krishnamurthi as well as his brother Nityananda (a different Nityananda from the guru of Muktananda) . . . Krishnamurthi became so mentally disturbed by his brother's death that he himself could not become the medium . . . But this world is a big drama: this experiment was done by great powers. The drama was played on an international scale by powerful individuals. When the possibility of Maitreya entering into Krishnamurthi became very near, certain, the soul of Devadatta, who had been Buddha's cousin, and who had for his whole life opposed Buddha and attempted several times to kill him, influenced the mind of Krishnamurthi's father (legally to repossess his son from the movement) . . . But on the higher plane, a great battle was fought between two powerful souls . . . Theosophists had gathered some 6,000 people in Holland from all over the world, and it was scheduled to be announced that Krishnamurthi had on that day given up his own personality and accepted that of Maitreya . . . But nothing happened. At that crucial moment, Krishnamurthi refused to relinquish his individuality . . . a great experiment failed.'[5]

Here indeed was quite an inner-plane account. It would influence some in the audience to jettison the clothing of their country to don the red robe and inherit a quasi-divine Indian name. Imagine Rajneesh's Western counterpart taking over the Grand Angus Commune Ranch of Wyoming and giving Indian pilgrims names like John Bunyan, Ralph Waldo Emerson, Saint Francis of Assisi and then giving them ten-gallon hats and holstered forty-four magnums, rawhide bull whips, while putting them on a diet of chitlins, pancakes, beans and steaks. They could read all about Pat Garrett and Billy the Kid. They could get 'Ram tough' by the campfire, where with ukulele they could sing *The Yellow Rose of Texas*.

But lest the saffron horde and assorted seekers get too raptured with these revelations about 'the externalization of the ascended Masters in the cosmic hierarchy', Rajneesh puts a damper on the value of his teachings. Many times he brags about being consistently inconsistent. He also lets another fact leak out:

'You need lies just like children need toys. Toys are lies. You need lies if you are not grown up. And if there is compassion, the person who has deep compassion is not going to be bothered whether he tells a lie or the truth . . . All Buddhas have lied. They have to because they are so compassionate . . . The whole truth will be too much. You may simply be shocked, shattered. The whole truth you cannot contain. It would be destructive. Only through lies can you be brought to the door of the temple. And only at the door can the whole truth be given to you. But then you will understand, then you will understand why the lies.'[6]

It was the coveted private evening darshan. A far more select group appeared. The inner circle, those with very special needs, and those now to be initiated as sannyasins. The buzzer rang and people rushed down the winding path towards Chuang Tzu Auditorium, in the private residence of Rajneesh, the Lao Tze house. Rajneesh sat on his throne in the marble hall. When he initiated, a throng of women stood up, swayed ecstatically, and danced around. His closest girlfriend, Ma Yoga Viveka, with whom he slept, acted as his *shakti*, his battery. Those waiting to be initiated nervously sat at the back waiting for their names to be called and then they knelt at Rajneesh's throne.

Rajneesh disclosed a part of the mystery of initiation:

'Whenever a Master wants to help you, cleanse your energy channels, your passage (*kundalini* spinal channel) if it is blocked, he simply possesses you. He simply descends into you and his energy which is of a higher quality, purer, unbounded, moves into your energy channels . . . This is the whole art of *Shakti-pat* (when he touches the forehead at initiation). If the disciple is really surrendered, the Master can possess him immediately. And once you are possessed by the energy of the Master, once his *prana* surrounds you, enters you, much is done very easily which you cannot do in years . . . But if a Master can enter you like a waterfall, many things are washed away. And when the Master has gone out of you, suddenly you start to be a totally different person.'[7]

This night a German housewife, a Japanese student, a mining engineer from New Zealand, a dress designer from Italy, and a French TV producer were to take sannyas along with a host of others. It was Susan's turn as well. She was trying fruitlessly to break her addiction to heroin.

She walked up and sat at his feet nervously when her name was called. Rajneesh told her to raise her hands up as if she were a tree swaying in the breeze. She closed her eyes at first. She sat in front of him, her heart racing. She barely breathed, and gazed at him in stillness. An incredible energy flowed between them. He was her father, her lover, her god. She worshipped him. Nothing in the world existed but she and Bhagavan. His energy poured into her, melting her.

'Sannyas,' he was telling her, 'is a new birth. Tomorrow you will be one day old. Sannyas has to take you to a new plane of being, a new level of consciousness. The new name is symbolic of being born again. I am giving you the name of Krishna so that you can make your life a celebration, a dance . . .'

She nodded, then told him she was a junkie, still on opium but not shooting heroin at least. She told him more.

'Have you tried to stop before?' he asked.

She nodded. 'About a dozen times.'

'Hmmmmmmm.' Rajneeesh closed his eyes, seeming to disappear. He returned with an answer.

'That is the trouble with trying to force yourself to break a habit, any habit. Whether it's alcohol or drugs or smoking . . . The habit will come back . . . Don't force yourself to stop taking drugs. Continue, but now be conscious of what you are doing and be conscious of the effect it is having on you. Don't fight it, just be conscious of it, of the whole process. Then by and by the habit will drop of itself. And you do some groups, hmmmmm? They will be helpful.'

He was referring to his secret therapy groups which Indians and non-sannyasins were generally not allowed to participate in. She bowed down to touch his feet as he said 'good' to her. She stood, 'shakily, wobbly, both her feet had fallen asleep, and stumbled back to her place. When she sat down, she suddenly found herself surrounded by a dome of stillness, enveloped by it. Made whole.'[8]

Susan would be one of many to enter the fold. And this would only be the beginning of her deep internal changes. As the energy reached fever pitch, through other initiations, Rajneesh at his throne, staring into the souls of those before him, touching their foreheads, and surrounded by dancing women, would resemble an antiquarian woodcutting of the horned-god, the goat of Mendes, at a midnight Sabat at Stonehenge, where women danced at his throne in the moonlight initiations. Not far from the horned-god of witchcraft would be a human sacrifice in waiting. But not so with these initiates. No. No.

As has been said, the layers of the onion only reluctantly fall away, as disclosures are rationed out. What has he said about his deep work within the communal experiment?

'My commune will become hidden, underground. It will have a facade on the outside: the weavers and the carpenters and the potters . . . that will be the facade. People who will come as

137

visitors, we will have a beautiful showroom for them . . . They can be shown around: a beautiful lake, swimming pools, a five-star hotel for them, but they will not know what is really happening. That which will be happening will be almost all underground. It has to be underground, otherwise it cannot happen.

'I have a few secrets to impart to you, and I would not like to die before I have imparted them to you—because I don't know anybody else now alive in the world who can do that work. I have secrets from Taoism, secrets from Tantra, secrets from Yoga, secrets from Sufis, secrets from Zen people . . . I have lived in almost all the traditions of the world . . . This is going to be a very secret work. Hence, Ajit Saraswati, I cannot speak about it. I think I have already spoken too much! I should not have said even this. The work will be only for those who are utterly devoted . . . But the real work is going to be absolutely secret.'[9]

'If we cannot create the New Man in the coming twenty years, by the end of this century, then humanity has no future . . . the third world war is going to be a global suicide. It can be avoided only if a new kind of man can be created. This is going to be an experiment, a great experiment, on which much is going to depend . . . This ashram is only just a launching pad. On a small scale. I am experimenting. The new commune will be on a big scale: ten thousand sannyasins living together as one body, one being. Nobody will possess anything: everybody will use, everybody will enjoy. Everybody is going to live as comfortably, as richly, as we can manage, but nobody will possess anything . . .'[10]

As has been said, one of the key innovations of this guru above the others is his synthesis of advanced contemporary psychological techniques in the peeling off of layer after layer in the onion-skinned defenses of his disciples—rolfing, rebirthing, primal scream, encounter groups, sex encounters, the deprivation tank, and so on. And then synthesizing this with *kundalini* yoga, *shakti-pat*, and far more subtle and esoteric forms of possession, mind-bending, and hidden initiations geared at blowing apart that most basic barrier, the barrier of the conscience, the sense of good and evil. Here is where Advaita and Tantra remain supreme. Not the popularized Tantra, but the cryptic North Indian Kashmiri variety. Here is where all the seals of what we

138

call a human being are blown apart.

Imagine once again the cat and the orange lizard—a microcosmic event indeed.

20

SPACE-RAIDERS AND PAC-MAN IN THE KUNDALINI ARCADE

It was now late spring, 1981, months following that first intense week in Poona. Martyn, Ada and Michelle had faded out of the picture and were back working with the Dilaram House in Calangute, Goa. I had been back in Poona regularly, five or six times, now staying with local friends, from four days to two weeks per jaunt. I would journey back and forth on the Deccan Queen from Bombay's Victoria railway station. Bombay had always been a central operating point for me in India.

One of my friends with whom I happened to stay in Poona was Ian Coltart, the superintendent of Poona's large modern Wadia Hospital. He was a sharp-minded Scot who had lived in India fifteen years. He was utterly fascinated by the phenomenon of Rajneesh, especially since his medical staff had access to inside information from local colleagues and specialists, who treated not only hundreds of sannyasins, but Rajneesh himself. Rajneesh's allergist for instance was Doctor Bapatt, a friend of a friend. I had a spacious verandah room with a balcony over-looking the central compound of Wadia Hospital. And numerous members of the medical staff had come to confide in me. As I suspected, many of them were intimidated by the strong-arm tactics of the Rajneesh Foundation.

Rajneesh had already begun his 'final phase' of silence. He was no longer giving lectures, and in fact was rarely appearing for darshans. Poona's heat was on the increase. A quiet transition seemed in effect. Meanwhile I was doing some front work for Uli Kohler, director of the Dilaram House in Goa, to get a branch started in Poona, a sort of halfway house for the countless dregs and casualties of the ashram. By now I was in touch with a number of local rescue operations, all of them Christian. Jane Dingle of the New Life Center was back in England, but she had spent years working with scores of maimed and bruised sannyasins. So had John and Val Maine, whose headquarters were on General Bhagat Marg, and with whom I had often stayed. Another of the more diligent of the workers among this damaged horde was Sister Miguela, who for seven years was one of the few who had access to all of the Poona hospitals, including the now off-limits Poona asylum.

Sister Miguela was a shy old nun from Spain who had lived in India thirty years. Deeply sad inflections haunted the rich Castillian accent of her voice as she narrated her tales. It was not easy meeting her. Finally I met her alone in the convent reception room. She saw few visitors, but she knew of me because of my book, which she had seen on the stands. My notoriety and my standpoint served to clear away any inhibitions she or any of the doctors had in confiding in me. Sister Miguela told me that she prayed for me because of what I had done through my book.

Tales of woe resounded through the polished marble corridor of the modern convent. One tragedy after another. It was like a Renaissance voice narrating the story of Romeo and Juliet. For she was telling me the tragic tale of Isabella, member of the Spanish royal family, a daughter of great promise who had cast her youth at the throne of Rajneesh.

'She was mad about him, crazy with Rajneesh. And she was jealous always of his girlfriend, Viveka, that pretty German girl. But Rajneesh all the same used her and tossed her out. He had relations with her. Then told her to have an affair with somebody she did not want. She could speak five languages, play the cello as a professional . . .'

Sister Miguela's voice trailed off.

'She wrote the most eloquent poetry in Spanish and Italian. She could quote you all of the classics. Her family wrote me again and again to talk sense into her, to get her back. She had cut them off, a common practice with the Rajneeshies. When they flew to India to see her, she would not even see them.

'Finally she was wasting away and would not eat. She began to dance madly in the park. They arrested her, then put her in the

141

Poona asylum. The ashram disclaimed responsibility for her, even disclaimed knowing her, saying she was not a true sann-yasin. That broke her. But she kept believing in Rajneesh, saying that this was all his test of loyalty. He was orchestrating these events. That he was . . .'

The nun paused to shudder. '. . . God! I tell you, he is the devil.'

She was choked with emotion.

'She was a fragile bird and he crushed her, her mind, her spirit, her body. He would say the most cruel things to her imaginable. And she was one of his inner circle, one of his oldest devotees, one of his closest. She had given him everything.

'Finally when I visited her I could no longer make sense out of what she was saying. She looked terrible in the asylum, babbling nonsense. I don't know when but I think they let her go. The authorities at the asylum have closed the records on her and will not talk about her. Some claim they don't ever remember having a patient with her name. I don't know where she is. I suspect she is dead.

'And you know what happened to her boyfriend? She finally got an Indian boyfriend before she went downhill. He too was close to Rajneesh, an Indian sannyasin. He had a great injury, maybe a broken leg. Then when he was in the general hospital, an unexplained disease was wasting him away. I saw him but he never wanted to talk to me. He asked me how she was. He told me he had made the mistake of his life in giving Rajneesh some contract on his soul, but now he could not get out of it. He had lost the will to live. The nurses would put in the glucose needle, and he would pull it out when they left him. He was from a wealthy Indian family. But finally he was out of money. And they just left his stretcher in the hall. He told me he was going to be in the morgue—that Rajneesh was putting a death spell on him.'

She stopped to get her breath.

'Well . . . I went to the hospital the very next day and looked all over and could not find him.

'They said they had no record of him . . . did not remember him. I knew some of those orderlies and they knew that I knew. I asked them where he went and they would not say anything. Finally I got one of them to admit that he was in the morgue, dead! Is that the liberation Rajneesh gives them? The terrifying thing about all these people is that they knew of their destruction and they could not stop it. They could not do a thing about it. They watched their own lives bleed out of them and all they could do was look on helplessly. I have seen too many cases like this. It is strange, devilish. It is a deep curse.

'Many of them have an obsession with suicide. An irresistible urge.'

Sister Miguela narrated a story I had already heard from one of the doctors. An Australian had recently committed suicide in one of the Poona hospitals. He dived off the balcony and broke his back. A voice of Rajneesh told him to do it. He had to obey the voice in an instant to achieve enlightenment. He lived through that, but when he tried again, it killed him. At night he would wail in the most uncanny manner. 'It sounded like the voice of hell.' He had even told her he was trapped and could not do anything to get out of it. He refused to listen to anyone. I acquainted the sister with one of Rajneesh's sayings in *A Madman's Guide to Enlightenment* (Darshan Diary, 1978):

'A moment comes when either you commit suicide or you become enlightened! That moment is precious, and that's where the master is needed, otherwise people WILL commit suicide.'

It was in black and white. The sister asked rhetorically,

'What happens if this so-called Master is not around, or is asleep, or refuses to come, or forgets you, huh?'

She continued with the story of the Australian.

'Do you know what happened when his mother came for the burial? Within two weeks she became a sannyasin! Can you believe this level of blindness?'

The sister asked me to end our session with a prayer.

As I drove off from the convent in a motor rickshaw, I felt an obsessive urgency to pursue this when I met with the doctors soon. I wanted to have the meeting that night. I couldn't wait.

Medical roundtable
Ian Coltart, superintendent of Wadia Hospital, had arranged for me to have a roundtable discussion with several very concerned doctors in the community. He also had lined up a private meeting with a man who had refused to talk to anyone so far. He was a

well-known Poona psychiatrist whose life had been threatened by the ashram if he divulged any of his knowledge regarding their operations that he had discovered from sannyasins who had snapped and were under his treatment. 'Snapped' is the word they used. It sounded like a sapling being broken near the roots and destroyed irreparably.

I sat in a private meeting with a small circle of doctors, mostly from Wadia Hospital. Our meeting was several days after my private meeting with the nun, Sister Miguela.

'It sounds like what we call a shooting gallery, or video arcade,' I told the doctors. We were discussing what happens behind closed doors on the ashram in the different groups. Some rooms were padded, some were locked. It was in one of these that Prince Welf of Germany was given his mortal wound.

What I was really after was a leak from someone from the inner circle, sworn to secrecy, under psychiatric treatment—one who because of insanity would divulge sworn secrets in his babblings to a doctor nearby or a probing psychiatrist. But no one in this present group knew what to look for. They were shocked enough at the 'ordinary' events in the Encounter and Tao groups. Rajneesh's highest male disciples ran these groups with an iron fist. They claimed to be mediums through whom Rajneesh worked.

The top group leader was a sinister-looking Englishman named Teertha whose pictures in the magazines invariably had him looking on voyeuristically at one assault encounter after another. He resembled Rasputin. He had been the European founder-director of Quaesitor, when he was still named John Lowe. It was Europe's largest human-encounter institute. He had also been a well-known encounter-group therapist in California in the sixties. But things did not go far enough to suit him in the American climate of conventional mores. So he left California disgusted. He met Rajneesh in the early seventies in North India, and was initiated immediately. He was now being groomed as Rajneesh's successor should Rajneesh die. Rumor had it he had gone to Oxford. He was also an advanced psychic, able to read people like the pages of a book and tear them apart before they knew what had hit them. He took a kind of glee in this, disarming every human defense conceivable and unearthing all and everything

144

within people. No region in the human psyche was sacred or private enough to evade his ruthless probes.

Rajneesh had been asked by a frightened woman disciple why he permitted Teertha the freedom to do anything in these groups with such savage authority. His answer was,

'I only send people to the Encounter group when I see that now they understand that they have to go beyond all boundaries—boundaries of sex, boundaries of violence, anger, rage. They have to break all the boundaries.

'That is breakthrough—when all those boundaries break down . . . But don't go on writing me. Whatsoever happens here is happening with my knowledge. Not a single thing happens here which is not known to me. So you need not inform me about things; I know them already. It is a sheer waste of time. And the moment you surrender and become an initiate, a sannyasin, that surrender has to be total . . . And nobody except me knows what the hidden pattern is. So you cannot go to Laxmi; she does not know. She simply asks me what is to be done and she does it.'[1]

He then told her that to be part of the commune, she would have to relax and stop judging.

Of course not everybody did stop judging. Richard Price, famed founder of Essalen, later repudiated his sannyasin status. He wrote the ashram a private letter that was later published in the Indian and American media (23 Feb 1978),

'The ashram encounter group is an abomination—authoritarian, intimidating, violent—used to enforce conformity to an emerging orange new order . . .'

Price mentioned specifics.

'A woman who had her arm broken was repeatedly kicked. A young man twice hit a sixty-year-old woman in the face. There were eighteen fights in the first two days alone—then I stopped counting. I did prevent one young man from hitting a sixty-one-year-old man with his fist. Stopping him was strictly against the 'rules'. After the end of the 'Encounter' group, a woman in the so-called 'Primal' group had her leg broken. On inquiry many other incidents came to light—injuries physical, mental, and spiritual.'[2]

One sannyasin, named Eckart Flother, was the senior editor of the magazine *German Business Week*, and ghost writer for a

German Prime Minister, as well as business consultant and leader of popular seminars. He had finally fled Poona heading a wave of other defecting sannyasins.

Eckart had seen a lot in Encounter groups. One thing really got to him. It was during the 'Samarpan' group in July 1978. The leader was an Englishman. And one of the girls in the group was wailing in remorse. Her parents had died and she could not get over the loss, the mourning. The leader pulled it out of her, her grief. By then all of them in the group were in the nude. She shook with tears. He had to thrust her through the shock barrier. He laughed, and told the group, speaking to her, 'all you need is sex'. She recoiled. He pushed her, made the group surround them in the circle. The group watched as the girl choked on her tears and the group leader raped her against her resistance. For Eckart it was horrible, it was too much. It was getting at his conscience. Then, not long after, another woman in the group was raped by two other group members. The leader permitted them to proceed. Again the group looked on like dogs in an alley. The leader pointed out that this had a therapeutic effect on the woman's inhibitions. (This is from a personal face-to-face testimony.)

Later Eckart, who was beginning to see more and more parallels to Hitler's Germany, would be stunned by such statements by Rajneesh as,

'Whatsoever you are doing consciously, with alertness, fully aware, becomes meditation. Even if you kill someone consciously, while fully conscious, it is meditative. This is what Krishna was saying to Arjuna: "Do not be afraid. Do not be afraid! Kill, murder, fully conscious, knowing fully that no one is killed . . . you are only destroying forms, not that which is behind the forms. So destroy the forms." If Arjuna can be so meditatively aware, then there is no violence. No one is killed, no sin is committed.'[3]

It smelled to Eckart a little like *Mein Kampf*.

Yet what baffled Eckart were the immense ecstasies he had experienced. But just because they were ecstasies, did that mean they had God's seal of approval? He knew then that heroin is supposed to be the supremely euphoric ecstasy. Who could deny the incredible desirableness of it? Did that make it good? One

146

had to look a little deeper, at the fruits, the effects. Those on the needle, as he had seen many times in Berlin and Munich, wasted away into atrophied husks. They had bombed their nervous system. Then perhaps a spiritual experience of the sweetest bliss might have parallels with heroin? After all, Eckart had 'blissed-out' after he had gone through an ashram 'enlightenment in-tensive'. With that spiritual experience, how could something that seemed so good co-habit on an ashram with experiences that appeared so evil? Rape and *samadhi* side by side? It was baffling.

After all, what had brought him to India as a skeptical journalist was the inexplicable 'cosmic orgasm' he had while standing up during a Rajneesh marathon session in Germany. It was a weekend session, he was doing one of the meditations, and for the first time in his life he felt waves and waves, crescendos and waterfalls of an incredible spiritual force. And this stayed with him for days. It was so powerful, so convincing, that Eckart resigned his job with the prestigious *Business Week* magazine. All of a sudden, conventional life seemed empty, flat, a dead drama. It was not long before he packed his stuff and left. You could say that he was taken in by degrees. Here was an intelligent, successful man who had suddenly been bombarded by an ex-perience and now life seemed empty without it. He was an agnostic caught unawares. And he seized it with a zest. The philosophical problem of evil seemed a moot point. It all looked good.

And his euphoria had come in a group context. Perhaps the secret, he told himself for months, was somehow to get through the dark moments in the groups. Then the euphoria would come in a greater dosage.

In one group epiphany, a sannyasin named Veda attended the 'Urga' group lead by Sagarpriya. It involved a kind of spon-taneous surrender of body movement. Then it happened,

'Veda felt a current of electricity pass through his body like a shock. From his right hand that was holding the left hand of a fat baldheaded man, through his body, out of his left hand and into the hand of the girl next to him.'

Veda was a Welsh poet who had been to Oxford.

'Before his mind had a chance to figure out what was happen-ing, it was there again. A bolt of electricity passing through his body. Passing from one person to the next, moving around the circle, coming back to him.'

The group began shaking violently.

'It was as if they were all possessed, taken over by a powerful, impersonal energy.'

He began to panic and pulled away from the circle.

'Confused, incredulous. Feeling that there was something that he had to try to understand, but not knowing what it was, not knowing where to look for understanding . . . His head began to throb. What was going on? The room was like a lunatic asylum. What was he doing there? Where was he? Was he on the outside looking in, or on the inside looking out? "Help!" he started screaming. "Help, help, help!" '[4]

But this was a lightweight group session. They got much more intense in the some thirty-plus group sessions, running from *shiatsu* massage to the full-blooded violence of the Encounter groups. Yet all of these groups were open to any sannyasin, and were still primary level. They were an indication of what was possible in Rajneesh's universe of experiences.

The Lila group was a medium-level group whose leader, Somendra, was one of a number of formerly famous Western therapists who had surrendered their lives to Rajneesh. Now things were changing configuration so fast, compared to proto-types in the West, that they were breaking pioneering ground daily. The Indian doctors and I would examine the report of a case in point:

Somendra had the reputation for being one of the best group leaders on the ashram. No one left his groups unscathed or unchanged . . . 'Okay, take your clothes off,' Somendra told the group, 'and stand in the corner over there.' They did, some shyly, others matter-of-factly. 'Move closer together so your bodies touch each other.' They did. Marsha made sure she was as far away as she could be from a certain acquaintance. 'Shakti!' Somendra yelled. 'Go into the opposite corner of the room.' A girl in her twenties with long, straight, blond hair . . . walked slowly to the opposite side of the room. 'Face the others and tell them your name.' She did. It wasn't loud enough. He screamed at her again.

'My name is Shakti,' she said.

'They can't hear you,' Somendra yelled.

'My name is Shakti,' she screamed.

'Louder,' he yelled.

'My name is Shakti.'

'Louder!' he bellowed.

Then she blew a valve . . .

'My name is Shakti, my name is Shakti, my name is Shakti.'

She was yelling at them enraged, trembling in the nude at this group of onlookers. Part of the trick was to elevate the group energy level. Somendra knew what to look for. He went over to Shakti.

Somendra told Shakti to breathe deeply through her belly. He began rocking her body back and forth at the pelvis. Suddenly her body was shaking and shaking, she was screaming. Somendra was moving around her—touching her on the back of her neck, on the chest, on the belly. As he'd touch her, his hands vibrating with energy, the part of her body where he touched her would begin shaking more and more violently. Shaking and screaming and crying—she became a dynamo of energy, a power plant gone haywire. She was on fire, she was about to explode. From the opposite corner they could feel her energy . . . some of them began shaking gently, some began crying. This was only the beginning of the group.

Next was a former fashion model. Somendra screamed her name. Her lean, angular model's body, attractive in clothes, looked ugly, Shiva noticed, when she was undressed . . . she looked grotesque . . . Yet despite the hard core of steel that seemed to run through her being, her body began shaking, tears dropped slowly from her eyes. Somendra, playing with her left nipple, began talking to her in rapid-fire staccato words that she could only understand in snatches because of his very heavy English accent.

'. . . You're not alive. You're a phony. You're the biggest phony I've ever seen. Look at yourself: you can't even cry. Everyone else can cry but you don't even know how to. Your tears are phony. I don't believe them. I don't think you have any feelings, I think you're dead inside. No life runs through your veins. I could choke you to death.' (His hands were fluttering near her throat). 'And you wouldn't even call out, you'd let me

149

do it. And you think that's what surrender is, what acceptance is. You don't know the first thing about surrender or acceptance.'

Both of them were acting out this drama in the nude in the center of the room. Somendra the group leader then barked at her,

'Go back into the corner,' giving her a hard, disgusted look. 'I can't work with you. You're not ready for it.'

And on through the group he went, cutting through them like a buzz-saw.[5]

The language would become more and more pornographic, as taboos were systematically shattered. People's minds would bounce all over the place. It became for some a kind of shock-orgasm. Abuse and degradation would deepen in new and more creative ways. This was liberation with a vengeance. The groups usually spent days and days locked up together with no escape.

It was exactly the kind of experimenting that Charles Manson did on his girls and his gang. When they had gang orgies, it was the same sort of thing as on the ashram. The Manson girls were making love with God and the Devil at the same time, wrapped up in one man, Charlie Manson. That is what he claimed and that is what they believed. In time, the Manson girls really got into blood-bathing it with victims. Blood and guts nailed to the walls. Huge meat-axes wailing away at flapping arms. And that is where Tantra, in its ancient tradition, takes you. The Tantric initiations are ultra-violent, ultra-perverse. And there is an ancient method in their madness. It has a lot to do with 'Explosion'. Ramakrishna, the Bengali super-guru, went through a certain Tantric phase. Not the violence. No. But the necrophilia, yes. He did meditate on dead bodies. He did a lot of things. Because he seemed so moral, it was cast in a moral light.

Other Bengali Tantrics blew the roof off morality totally and put Ramakrishna's meager experiments to shame. I noticed that, on my return trip to Poona, *Onlooker* Magazine and several other Indian magazines were printing very daring exposés of Tantra. And they kept going back to death and human sacrifice, as a central focus. If you really want to raise the energy level, you whack somebody to pieces in an occult context. Alistair Crowley observed the same hidden wisdom. It is a progression.

Teertha's groups were far more violent than Somendra's. And

he was more ruthless. The more sensitive souls feared them. But when Rajneesh ordered them to go, they went. Love made amazing demands. For these explorers of consciousness were pioneering new and daring redefinitions of the word 'Love'.

Not that Teertha would disclose much. For these were groups for the elementary sannyasins at large. And his statements were held up to public scrutiny. So he had to be cautious. Still, he divulged a morsel:

'Practically everybody's violent, practically everybody. Very rarely is a man not angry. In the most violent thing we ever had in the group, the man went into *samadhi* (enlightenment) afterwards. He wanted to Kill somebody! Oh, he was killing somebody, he was killing him, and the group couldn't stop him. Then he threw the whole group off, and then he got this person and hung him up on the wall . . .

'Yeah, and nobody could stop him. They were hitting him and kicking him, and nothing could stop him. And then I just said, "Stop it. Turn the energy inside." And he went into *samadhi*. Just like that. But he was killing. That was the most violent. He swung the furthest that way, gave it up, and swung the other way. And anything half-hearted doesn't work. The sex in the group, fighting and sex and jealousy and all, they're all peripheral. They're all methods of raising the energy. And unless the energy comes up . . . nothing can be done with a dead person . . . nothing affects him.'

Energy was increased by these incredible, taboo-shattering acts. This was pure Tantra.

Asked about the ceiling of limitation on such experiments, Teertha disclosed,

'The limits are endless. And I don't know what they are. I just know it's an open tunnel. And no matter how far we go down it, we don't even see the end. Yes, it's just endless. Bhagavan's just . . . he is just endless . . . But now looking at Bhagavan, he's just an example of the endlessness, of just how far we can go. We're not working under a ceiling, we're not working to a limit, it is just absolutely limitless. And that's what we seem to discover in each group; it seems the more we let go, the further it goes.'[6]

The doctors and I shared these accounts back and forth growing in horror as the import of it all kept hitting us. There was really no end to them. We were all probing together, looking, examining the pattern, Ian Coltart and the several physicians and I.

'What has to be remembered,' I said, 'is that these groups are the entry-level initiation, beginners class. You can't start blowing the seals within the interior of the soul in the deeper regions until the initiate can become blasé about the lesser taboos of good and evil, such as rape and assault and perversion.'

I had to say this to the doctors to make sense out of why Rajneesh was doctoring Tantra for Westerners using psycho-therapeutic models. They were not unfamiliar with Tantra. But most of them were non-Hindus, Christians, hence the shocked reaction. It is more shocking when you are there seeing the damage. Hearing about it is tertiary. They had certainly seen and heard the after-effects.

There is a certain flavor to a direct apprehension, watching someone fall apart in your arms, a lovely, helpless Western girl who has had too much—that, the Indian doctors had seen count-less times. They weren't sure why these affluent foreigners were such suckers for punishment. Though at the same time, India had been completely accepting of the most horrendous initiations among its Hindus since time immemorial.

It was just that up close with Westerners it all felt a little odd. They knew that with a trip to Benares you could see anything . . . but here, with so many broken victims? It somehow computed differently in their minds when compared to the so-commonly-reported national religious perpetrations that were even more shocking: commonplace rituals of this day and age—Bengali child sacrifices to Kali (MahaDurga), village dismemberments to gods in Mysore, babies sacrificed all over India when a dam or a bridge is built. Everyday affairs.Those victims somehow seemed lesser people than these well-to-do, full-blooded foreigners. Or did the change in imagery restore the evil for what it was by changing the spotlight of focus, by substituting white men for primitive villagers?

Days later I saw, privately, the psychiatrist whose life was threatened. Rarely have I seen anyone so afraid. He was truly in a cold sweat. He did not want us to mention his name to anyone. He was very reluctant to talk about anything. But what he knew seemed terrible enough. Ian Coltart assured him that his story would be on file, should he disappear, as a vindication, that he should not die fruitlessly. He should be apprehensive enough about the evil present to want to stop it in the lives of others.

'Have you heard of many suicides among the sannyasins?' I pressed him. He nodded nervously.

'Yes, many.'

'How many?'

'It's hard to tell. Fifty, sixty, hundreds?'

'And murder?'

'Well, if they will threaten my life . . . and I know people, I am a psychiatrist, and they mean it . . . Then what is to prevent them killing whom they choose? Yes, they have murdered, that I know.'

'But do they do it for fun? Or do it for ritual? Do you think . . .'

The psychiatrist looked at the floor sadly.

'I can't prove their motives entirely. It is very probable . . . almost certain.'

'Okay,' I pressed, 'what does Rajneesh do with the inner circle. Does he do any really heavy Tantric stuff like human sacrifices or sex with the dead? Have any of your 'snapped' patients mumbled anything about this, patients who were close to Rajneesh?'

He sat in a cold sweat, dripping, looking at the floor. He was a very frightened man. And obviously he wished he had never in his life heard the name of Rajneesh. He did not answer my question, he changed the subject, which according to Indian custom means an end to questioning.

'My family has lived in Poona for generations. I just don't want to leave. My mother lives here. Besides, if I leave, they can track me down, they can always track me down.'

After the goldrush

Then several weeks later, we got a phone call. I thought of the relief the psychiatrist would feel when we told him the news. The night of 30 May, Rajneesh's Rolls Royce quietly rolled out of the ashram late at night, past midnight, and sped to the Poona airport where they had a plane waiting for him. He would connect with a Pan Am 747 headed for the States. It would fly out, as many international flights do, at two-thirty in the morning. Rajneesh's car would be driven into the hold of that plane or one folllowing it. Like other Indian godmen, he would board the plane like a king, being taken up a separate entrance with seventeen inner-circle sannyasins. He reserved the entire first-class compartment, and nobody was allowed in. Even days later the regular sannyasins on the ashram would not be told. Then a week later, the Indian papers would admit that they had evidence that Rajneesh had left the country . . . to Switzerland, or England, or America.

It was now after the goldrush. The mass departures were awesome. Bamboo villages were going up in flames. Items were being auctioned. And things were in utter confusion. Heart-broken and lost sannyasins wandered about in a daze. Broke, numb. Many had given their fortune to the foundation, and were not about to be reimbursed. They thought their security would be here, that this Indian niche would never dissolve. But it did. The New Holy City was to be in Antelope, Oregon, where within a year, 'God' would live on The Big Muddy Ranch, and own a long line of over forty Rolls Royces. The ranch, one might add, was where John Wayne and Katherine Hepburn filmed *Rooster Cogburn*.

Another thing started cropping up in the Maharashtra papers, then later the national papers—the alarming number of suicides amongst the sannyasins. The consulates in Bombay were going wild. But the drama was by no means over. The Rajneesh explosion was merely shifting arenas, and gathering momentum. He had, after all, made his ride to the harvest-field, America.

154

21

BRINGING ENLIGHTENMENT
TO COWBOY COUNTRY

For a while Rajneesh appeared on the American scene like the Wizard of Oz. The guru sat on his famous throne in flashing multi-colored clothing like a Walt Disney sorcerer as thousands in flame-red robes surrounded him within his own enchanted kingdom in the central desert of Oregon. But after four years of escalating controversy he left America like Legion, the biblical demoniac, on a package tour. He was being pursued by thirty-five federal indictments. This time the master was twitching and in chains before news cameras as North Carolina police with shotguns surrounded his private Lear Jet. He and those left within his inner circle were trying to refuel and escape the country. Again, a second time, Rajneesh had crept out the back door, but this time he was caught. He would not be able to leave America until he pleaded guilty to two indictments, paid a fine, and agreed never to return.

Within weeks of his arrival on the American scene, page-length pictures of Rajneesh ran in *Newsweek* and *Time* magazines week after week offering his pronouncements to the American culture. It was merely a matter of time until the biggest television news programs in the nation felt the pull of curiosity. *PM* magazine, *Nightline*, *Sixty Minutes*, *20/20* and nightly network news looked for Watergate-type clues behind the secretive cult. A game ensued to see who could probe beneath the elaborate security of Rajneesh's expanding commune. Like a decoy the sensationalism of the bizarre inevitably diverted the inquiries and they went no further.

With media preoccupation came the circus atmosphere. Rajneesh indulged America's voyeuristic quest for fantasy as he played the role of entertainer and stage director. Some of this was 'hi glam', as he accumulated a fleet of ninety-six Rolls Royces. The prestigious *San Francisco Chronicle* featured Rajneesh on the front page countless times. The commune became a movie set with Rajneesh's throne as the supreme director's chair. Describing the pageantry, the *Sunday/Chronicle Examiner* reported on the Third Annual World Celebration on 1 July 1984. On the front page was an awesome picture of the bearded guru on a huge stage before 15,000 followers. The shocker was that on each side of him were special disciples with semi-automatic assault rifles. The *Chronicle* described the event:

'Rajneesh arriving in a white Rolls-Royce accompanied by a security helicopter and two machine-gun-toting Rajneeshpuram police officers, made his first appearance of the festival during an hour-long morning worship service.

'Dressed in a long purple robe with gold glitter, the Bhagwan sat in a large padded chair on a raised platform before 15,000 disciples in Rajneesh Mandir, a 2.2 acre temple in the scenic valley of Rajneeshpuram.

'Thousands of worshippers bowed to a smiling Rajneesh as their long slow chants of "I go to the feet of the awakened one" echoed through the valley. As Rajneesh was sitting in the temple, two armed guards stood on each side of him . . . Later, as Rajneesh drove by his followers, a helicopter buzzed over the crowd. A man with an automatic weapon leaned out of the helicopter.'

There was no mistaking the scope of Rajneesh's operation and wealth. The *Chronicle/Examiner* commented that much of the festival participants' time was spent frolicking in Krishnamurti Lake, dancing in the Rajneesh Disco, playing blackjack in the Rajneesh Casino or sipping cocktails or iced cappucinos in the Zorba the Buddha lounge. Access was determined by arm-bands and plastic ID cards while closed-circuit TV cameras monitored everything.

Rajneeshpuram had been legally declared a city as 'dozens of new buildings have been constructed in the last two years in what Rajneesh officials say is a $100 million investment now'. This was a new order of power compared to Poona. If the defense system of Poona amounted to stun prods at the gate, here there were sophisticated machine-guns and helicopters in a far vaster commune in twentieth-century America. This time Rajneesh had over 120 square miles to play with backed by his own police force that was legally sanctioned by the State of Oregon.

There were echoes of the regime of Poona in Oregon but there was also something missing—that occult air of mystery and intrigue that haunts the ancient cities of India. That timeless feeling, with its soul-wrenching sense of the numinous that eternally lingered between the grotesque and the beautific of India, was not so readily transported to America. Not all of the circus props could be loaded into the 747.

Now the faithful worked fourteen hours a day building their millennial city. But at 2 p.m. every day the loyal sannyasins set down their hoes and hammers, left their cash registers in the Bhagwan's shopping mall, left their day jobs in the Casino Rajneesh to line Nirvana Drive for a peek at the Master driving by. He would drift by hypnotically in one of his ninety-six Rolls Royces. Above him were the fan blades of a big chopper. After *darshan* they couldn't just leave, as they did in Poona, and take rickshaws into town or sightsee or go to leisurely orgies. They were in the middle of a vast wilderness. This was a more sobering experience. What made it even more sobering was Rajneesh's present choice of the reigning witch in residence, Ma Anand Sheela, who in America replaced the one who ran the Poona ashram in India, Ma Yoga Laxmi. Sheela deftly excommunicated the former sannyasi boss of Poona during Laxmi's brief stay in Oregon, thus severing her last vestiges of power. The black widow had stung another rival.

Sheela was arrogant, ruthless, and ambitious, hostile and testy, daring everybody to take her on, even the Oregon government and local residents whom she had ejected from their small town of Antelope. These American ruralites she labeled 'retards'. She loaded the ballot box and seized local political control while behind her a sharp cabal of lawyers manipulated America's malformed legal system to make all things possible. Her fellow-disciples she humiliated and disdained as no more than mere peons in her realm. Clearly this was unthoughtful for a group utterly dependent on the devotion, funds, and loyalty of its following. She was biting the hand that fed her. She was also

157

beginning to seize a little too much power, crossing the threshold into her master's domain. *The Oregonian* reported that she told a lawyer during a court deposition, 'I am the head of the religion, and I request that you respect that and address me in same fashion.' Rajneesh alone had been due that honor, as he repeated in so many ways in the past.

When Sheela's time finally ran out, and she quietly left in one of Rajneesh's 737 jets from his own private airstrip, the commune exulted and celebrated. By then the American public loved hating Sheela. Within weeks she would be arrested and jailed in West Germany on charges of conspiring to murder a list of Oregonian officials and rival disciples including Rajneesh's long-term mate, Ma Yoga Viveka, who was one of the few to survive the political upheavals. On trans-Atlantic television the master and Sheela would call one another names. It was a cosmic lover's quarrel. But more wary minds wondered if this was not another *deus ex machina* to abscond funds to a Swiss account before the federal heat closed in. Was this more high theater to fool the United States inspectors and prepare the way for a big move? And where were the next Elysian fields?

Clearly Rajneesh's experiment in consciousness in America had become bent. His constant quest for utter privacy, where dark deeds can be done in total secrecy, now had the air of a super-porn peep show with a million eyes staring in. The magnitude of the planned obscenity could not reach its threshold. The delicate seed pod for the total experience—where Mephistopheles promised godhood through the subterranean encounter and pursuit of total evil—could not flourish under media badgering while feds slammed at the gates with arrest warrants and litigation. The Rajneesh corporate experiment resembled a sex-crazed couple forever in pursuit of a dark spot away from the frenzy of the streets to do their deeds while a noisy mob of paparazzi with flash cameras pursued them. As the lust craze grew more intense the noisy mob drew closer, gnashing at their heels. The final resort was a vast public obscenity with cripples and screaming infants looking on amidst a mob of twitching madmen, laborers, angry police, and deeply offended citizens. Sooner or later the guns and chains would come out. Frederico Fellini had invaded the Rajneesh set and a delicate brain operation was again beginning to resemble a lobotomy. Some privately wondered when the Hells Angels would appear on the Rajneesh set with chain saws and shotguns.

Rajneesh, forever mutagenic, trespassed on yet another of his vows. He broke his vow of silence and declared a world-wide press conference. In part he was ending Sheela's reign of power. Whatever had been bottled in during these four years of silence could not wait to get out. The *Sunday Chronicle/Examiner* of 21 July 1985, during the Fourth Annual World Festival, reported his controversial first utterances:

'Jesus Christ was a crackpot.'

'Only the retarded and utterly mediocre people can believe in God.'

'I am the best showman in the whole history of mankind. This is my circus, my carnival. And I enjoy it immensely.'

Media interest was not slack during this period. But the public feared a repeat of the Jim Jones event of Guyana when 900 committed mass suicide. Rajneeshpuram might be building up to something ballistic, news pundits warned. Meanwhile within four months of this Sheela had left.

During the interim time between Sheela's departure and the guru's, Rajneesh seemed to occupy the airwaves more than ever. He accused Sheela of murder and conspiracy, building underground tunnels and bugging the rooms, and, above all, absconding funds. He told his followers that they no longer needed to wear red. They burned books. And again his metaphysics underwent a change of wardrobe. As ever, it seemed to relate to the pressing agenda of the moment, above all, mounting state and federal legal charges against the guru. On national television, he told Ted Koppel, on *Nightline*,

'This is not a religion. I am not their guru or leader. I am only their friend. That is all.'

When asked about his earlier messianic claims and the enormous gifts of the faithful, he called them tokens of friendship.

Then came the one-dimensional demythologizing of the unknown by the experts. Often pop psychologists were brought forward on TV interviews to explain it all away with simple five-point explanations and urban insights. The burning center of the force eluded the interpretations of those who perceived events. Most often it came down to TV panels of specialists and academics in fencing matches. The consensus voice to the people was well-packaged and sage, rational, analytic, pragmatic, skeptical, and forever reductionistic. Yes, surely no one could deny that often such insights were compellingly true on at least a pedestrian level. But it often went no farther than a sociological packaged theorum given as an anodyne, a humanistic pacifier, for the public to satisfy further need for inquiry. America has a way of bleaching away mystery, leaving things sterile and flat like the formica in an operating room. But the ghost in the machine slipped away undetected. The experts saw the decoys, focusing in on the theater in the round, while their eyes were too diverted to catch the deft sleight of hand behind the scenes.

What compounded this was that suddenly Rajneesh was like one of the magicians in the court of Pharaoh who suddenly could do no more miracles when challenging Moses—a power source had been cut off. It was like the famed Krishnamurthi who in Switzerland in the 1920s projected vast blue auras that dazzled the crowds of Europe, but when he arrived in Hoboken Harbor, New York, his aura was flattened. So he left.

On 14 November 1985, in Portland, Oregon, Rajneesh pleaded guilty to two counts of the federal indictment, while the remaining thirty-three counts were dropped. He was given a ten-year suspended prison sentence, fined $400,000 and ordered to leave the United States, which he did that day. He arrived at New Delhi's International Indira Gandhi Airport on 17 November, where one of India's leading film stars acted as his chauffeur. He blistered America in an on-the-spot interview, promised to live in Mother India, where he could stay secluded in Himachel Pradesh's Kulu Valley, 'The Valley of the Gods', 250 miles north of Delhi. But that lasted no more than a month, when the guru headed for Nepal but only stayed there for a few weeks. By now Sheela was in a West German prison in Baden-Baden waiting to be extradited to the United States where she was to go on trial for attempted murder, conspiracy, wiretapping, and a local salmonella mass poisoning. The monetary center for the organization remained the Rajneesh Services International Ltd, the London corporation set up in 1982 as the world-wide financial umbrella. But now they faced outstanding debts to creditors and legal services upwards of 35 million dollars.

By early January of 1986 Rajneesh and a small group had moved to a Greek island where they lived in a mansion until the Greek Orthodox Church, inflamed by insults, demanded that the government eject the group for blasphemy and sexual orgies. An angry mob surrounded the house ready to stone it when the Greek government interceded. The mad package tour proceeded, this time to Heathrow Airport but they did not let Rajneesh go any further than the barrier. The cosmic road show then headed off to Ireland for a spell, then Switzerland. But they were deported each time. The goal now is a South Pacific island, perhaps even the one owned and offered by Marlon Brando. Then they may be free of all surveillance and all law, so that the most secret acts can be perpetrated in a grand orgy of occult alchemy. Perhaps then a final initiation will be performed, one that may pale anything the Master has done so far.

PART II
—THE EXPLOSION—
PERSPECTIVE TWO

22

THE GATE OF INITIATION

An old Harlem jazz artist named Lord Buckley used to say,
'If you get to some place, and you can't get back, then there you jolly well are, aren't you!'
And a mocking sax would wail away.
Another street-wise guru might say,
'If you take a look at yourself, compare yourself now to how you have been at the peak of life. Are you growing or shrinking? What's happening inside?'
After two years with Sai Baba, being among his select disciples, and being in his chemical laboratory, the bottom line was that I encountered one danger signal after another. I kept smelling hell out of the back door. A million Indians would have given anything to fill my shoes. By the end of two years with Baba, I had Indian Governors circulating my writings in different parts of India, I travelled among the elite, and I was one of a very few people in history to share a stage with Sai Baba, speaking in front of over twenty thousand influential Indian leaders who were just faces in the mob.

As mentioned previously, my own chronicles of this experience are so intertwined that any intelligible summary is difficult to relate. The occult transitions in my life during those years in India with Sai Baba take up a book twice the length of this one. And though they would be shocking and alien to many people, those on the path would see one familiar roadsign after another. We have space here to examine a few patterns. The ones that sit at the doorstep of the ego-death Explosion into 'Enlightenment'.

What I had to start looking for, since Explosion is a one-way mirror, were give-away signals of any kind. So often they appear in the major initiations in consciousness, when patterns begin to crop up and reappear. Those patterns have a strange recurrence.

An important event will hint at what I was going through. It was an occult vision-dream I had in the spring of 1971 when I was in the jungles of Mysore, thirty miles from Mysore city in the ancient locale of Sri Ranga Patna, whose ancient temple loomed into the silver-grey monsoon sky. I was writing my first book advocating Sai Baba. In the late afternoon I would swim in the Cauvery River, which flowed by my suite, or I would go to this ancient temple in the nearby town to meditate. The temple had once swarmed with shaven-headed Brahmin priests doing propitiations to the gods seven hundred years ago as they do today. Before Columbus discovered America, this temple was alive with activity, its gods imparting revelations and directions to the worshippers. Among these rites were human sacrifices to Vishnu—a huge black stone colossus reclining in the inner sanctum. Today it still reclines in the blackness and receives offerings from pilgrims.

I was a lone guest in a wilderness dak bungalow that the government had renovated. It had been the guest house of an Indian Maharaja, sitting off to the side of the jungle. It had a palatial festooned road.

It was here that I was trying to force my mind past the most recent barrier of resistance, which had not bothered me for several years. It was the old transition of saying, 'All things constitute the godhead, therefore I am part of godhead, therefore I AM God.' My recent resistance was the 'I AM God' part of the proposition. A haunting voice within me called it blasphemy, the old deception in the Garden of Eden. Creature calling itself God. I thought I had transcended this elementary stumbling-block that a non-dualist, an Advaitin, wrestles with. Maybe it was because I was approaching that final gate beyond which there is no return. And deep down I wondered,

'Is all this really true?'

Compounding this problem of resistance was the ancient temple with its multi-tiered, blackened layers of gods looming high into the ancient sky of India. At dusk the crimson streaks from the horizon gave an orange cast to the thousands of intertwined deities daisy-chained and dancing and beckoning from the rising stucco gate on up to the top throne of Vishnu, sixty feet in the air.

My 'test' was to get beyond seeing this as the idolatry that the biblical God condemns. And it was a problem. It was a problem reconciling the sublime genius of India's highest abstract mystical philosophies which grew up hand-in-hand with idolatry and human sacrifice. They were bedfellows, these two. And the fruit of what they had reaped on the land of India was not encouraging. The land was a wounded beast, travailing. For India fits the accursed description of Babylon with its mystery religions and its idolatry. Something in me wanted to make sure at the last moment, before I hurled myself on the funeral pyre of enlightenment.

Then in the early hours of one morning in the still quiet of the dak bungalow, bordering the jungle, I had an occult vision. And it shook me to pieces. I had to remind myself that the closer to the final leap an adept got, the more labyrinthine and titanic the tests to dissuade him. It was the analogy of the Tibetan Dragon—one wayward thought by the high-lama-turned-dragon, sitting at the bottom of an iced lake, and he would be sent back to the beginning of his quest, less than an amoeba. The closer to the gate, the bigger the stakes.

The occult vision

The vision is in the city of Cairo. Sai Baba has impelled me out of an inner-circle meeting to go down to the Cairo docks to a massive stone warehouse that is an ancient temple in disguise. It contains the monumental cryptic chambers of ancient Egypt. I enter one dingy doorway of a vast grey building composed of ten-ton seamless blocks that climbs without windows five stories high.

Inside the warehouse walls, hidden stairs lead up to the upper vaults. I ascend and enter upon the landing of ancient stone and am ushered by a guide to a doorway twenty feet high. It is directly from Thebes or Karnak. A power swings the door open, then swings it half shut behind me as I enter.

I join a chanting line of initiates in the dark shadows. They appear held in a powerful trance. We are all facing a high priest. The flickering light within comes from two black sulphur candles at an altar. They reveal the chamber to be quite large. The priest has a distinctly hooded appearance, like a sorcerer or Druid. His companion priest is now quite familiar. I recognize him to be the

167

principal of Sai Baba's Veda school in Puttaparthi, the little gnome-man with the burning eyes. The butterflies in my stomach are in a nauseous terror, sensing 'The anvil of choice', as I have always called it.

Standing above us at least fifteen feet high against the altar walls are two stone giants that can be found at either the British Museum or the tomb of Rameses the Second. They are Seth and Anubis, the Egyptian god of evil, and the jackal god of the necropolis of death. The priest holds a burning censor as something tells me that it is tanus leaves burning. The hypnotic chants become more intense.

I now see that to our left, behind thick curtains, are circular stairs that lead to an even higher upper chamber. I sense there is no way down. It is a one-way entrance. A priest has pulled open the curtains to beckon us on with a lit candle. Occult symbols flicker dimly in the background—pyramids, the all-seeing-eye.

With helpless terror I am close to losing my mind. For suddenly both granite giants, perhaps fifty tons each, have unglued themselves from the wall and are now starting to edge forward with hideous strength. The eyes blink open with yellow light like furnace doors raging within. The gigantic feet sound like hydraulic hammers each time they hit the rock floor. A wind has entered the room from nowhere.

Then as the others move behind me in a daze, I desperately calculate an escape. The priests move up the stairs as the two living statues slowly follow them. One statue stops and searches the initiates with a baleful power. It pulls at me like a tremendous magnet. My spirit fights my body not to proceed but to escape in the final waning moments of dim hope before my fate is sealed. It is much the same instinctive way that a field mouse automatically dodges the beak and talons of a hawk. Its reactions are inbuilt.

Then, a part of my mind feels the tug of a deep question,

'Why is it that every time I reach this same gate, this narrow choice of initiation, that no matter how light, airy, loving, and innocent the pathway has been, the doorway, the rite, cannot be made in any other fashion than that which is unbelievably sinister to my deepest feelings? Why does it bear a total resemblance to the very horrors that I most instinctively feared as a small child, the deepest things of Satan? Why does the predominant feeling have to be evil and not good? Or why can't it at least be a gray mixture in between? Why never the bells of bliss? For, at the final moment, the carpet is pulled from under you, and you still have to pass through the fire and kiss the feet of some demon god. And only then can you pass through the tunnel that you can never see the other side of.'

In the final possible moment, I suddenly gain control of my arms and legs after calling to Jesus Christ, of all the names in the cosmos. The force breaks. I plunge through the front door down the inner stairs with such nimble quickness that the somnambulistic procession cannot stop me.

Very soon after that, this very vivid, very unusual meditative occult experience came to a powerful end, and I spent the day thinking about it near the base of the ancient South Indian temple of Sri Ranga Patna. It was not just a dream. There was a familiar presence behind the machinery of appearances. It felt like a rehearsal of something I would soon be expected to go through.

The experience would be a vivid foreshadowing of an event between me and Sai Baba. Only it would be tangible this time. I could well see the parallel.

But as I packed to leave, the question that haunted me then was, Would I or would I not bow before this force and enter the unknown tunnel? And was the end of it heaven or hell? What was the clue? (The clue to what is the real consciousness on the other side of Explosion, beyond the point of no return.)

A very unsavory, unwelcome, 'unevolved' thought kept haunting me and would not go away. It was the matter of Demon Possession. What if on the other side of Explosion the process was not man becoming God at all? What if it was rather man being conned into emptying himself, because of his ambition to become God, and in the process hooking up with a vast demonic principality and intelligence that was masquerading as God-consciousness?

I had at certain rare times 'smelled' the void on the other side of the Explosion. I had in the sixties had my own taste of *nirvana* in an overwhelming experience in the wilds of the Virginia countryside. A number of gurus and pundits authenticated it, including Sai Baba. I went through a pinpoint of light, in the experience, into another universe of thought. I had for an atom of time entered what I termed 'the unborn, the ocean of being, the static-eternal beyond all names, forms, and language'. I document it in *Avatar of Night*. It was that which drove me into the Upanishads, and ultimately to sell everything I owned in order to move to India. It was that line of cosmic crumbs that drove me into the kingdom of Sai Baba, India's most powerful and illustrious guru. If anyone was superhumanly confident of his adeptship, his proximity to the kingdom of *nirvana*, it was I, Tal Brooke. Until . . . I smelled an ancient cold leaking out of the window into the void . . . the Explosion, the black hole.

What the astronomers call a black hole makes a good analogy for that same type of one-way barrier as Explosion. In a collapsed star that has become a black hole, gravity is of such magnitude that it sucks everything into itself. Imagine a gravity so vast that not even light can rise above the unspeakable pull. Light, which travels at fantastic speeds and has virtually zero mass, is overcome by the gravitic force. No light escapes.

When a guru, a Rider, emerges from Explosion, you have his revelations, his claimed experiences, and his non-human personality operating behind a poker face. Like a good screen actor, he can manipulate every button of human reaction, but behind it is a cold, unknowable, non-human intelligence. Who is the Rider? Who or what is occupying the body? Could it be something like the Dark Force impelling Darth Vader? He says he is one with God. He says a lot of things. Clearly, if he is truly Enlightened and has passed all the tests, he is an enigma within a riddle and you can either believe or disbelieve his claims. But make them he does. They all do, all the Riders—'I am God,' they say.

If we cannot peer into the black hole of the 'static-eternal' and are faced with the well-known psychologist's dilemma of assessing subjective private experience, we are forced into looking into a lot of associated areas. One key area lies in the initiatory signs, the flavor or essence of those signs, leading to the barrier of the Explosion. And we begin to see a pattern. The pattern may wrap itself in varying semantic packages, but the flavor is there. And this is true whether the initiation is Tantric, Mahayana Buddhist, by means of *kundalini*, *shakti-pat*, or the spontaneous

Explosion of Rajneesh in the garden at midnight under the maulshree tree, or Sai Baba's spontaneous and powerful character change.

Curiously, when the heavy-hitting gurus, the Riders, emerged from the Explosion, close associates and family usually used the term 'possession' in describing the change that they saw. Rajneesh prepares his highest adepts by readying them emotionally to do the same thing—sink into the infinite abyss, and drop away and keep dropping away. His words are a juggling act. Along with this comes the admonition, 'Don't worry about what fills you or enters you. Let it happen. Surrender. Lose your identity forever.'

The only scripture on earth that deals with this phenomenon is the Holy Bible. Period. It talks about massive evil intelligences operating behind the scenes of our world. It talks about Possession. It has live historical instances of demonic possession and exorcism.

But there is also a super-class in this group whose possession is different—it is a Perfect Possession and the consciousness within the possessed is many levels beyond the standard possessor-demons. This was all a revelation to me in India ten years ago, as I searched desperately for a category in which to put this phenomenon. Suddenly I noticed that this category of creatures repeatedly appears in the Bible's pages. The Bible even predicts, in its prophecy, that one day the world would be full of these creatures. What are they? Antichrists, claiming to be God! Their appearance and reign on the earth was prophesied to precede the Return of Christ. Why had I not seen it before?

I will never forget my thoughts at that time. I had discovered an absolutely Satanic thing operating behind Sai Baba's veneer. Now I was desperate. I crouched on a massive boulder on a hillside overlooking Baba's main ashram in Puttaparthi. My love affair with Vedanta was ending. I was dissolving inside, dying inside. I was a needle rolling on a thread. Soon after that, I would confront Baba publicly. In my perplexity, I was willing to look anywhere for an answer. There was one source of revelation I had avoided.

In my desperation, I laid a Bible on a hillside rock—a book I had long ago 'transcended'. Now in an act of faith, I threw open the pages. You could call it a kind of miracle at the time. What I read answered a need so deep I cannot explain it. For by then I was in a blackened state of mind best described as occult desolation. In trying to figure out this creature in the red robe, claiming to be God out here on the Indian desert, I was totally lost for an answer, bewildered.

Imagine what I felt when the Bible fell open to Matthew 24:23–24 (New International Version). It was Christ himself talking about a future age in our world. And suddenly a new perspective took shape for me:

'At that time if anyone says to you, "Look, here is the Christ," or, "There he is!" do not believe it. For false Christs and false prophets will appear and perform great signs and miracles to deceive even the elect—if that were possible. See, I have told you ahead of time.'

I looked down at Baba's green prayer hall below and thought, 'That's it, that's what Sai Baba is, a miracle-working antichrist.'

Miracles, according to what I had just read in the Bible, were not infallible proof that one was divine, or in touch with God-consciousness. Or had transcended time-space. No. The powers of evil could work miracles, and in fact would do so more and more as the 'Last Days' came to fruition in the world's history.

It became vivid, this new class of creatures—superhumanly-energized figures proclaiming to be God in human form, yet in a state of Perfect Possession. Not ordinary demonic possession, but perfect. The original human inhabitant now fully obliterated out of the body, blow-torched as it were. The new resident consciousness not your standard comic-book demon, but a massive, baleful intelligence that is ageless, that has witnessed cosmic creation, that is extremely powerful and extremely evil. The ultimate prototype of this creature yet to come on the earth is what St. John in his Revelation would term the final Antichrist. Only in this case the resident consciousness would be Satan himself, who would get most of the inhabitants of the world to worship him as God and surrender their souls to him. It may seem far removed—until you think about what is going on right now.

There really are Riders today—Sai Babas and Rajneeshes,

172

making the claim to Deity, of being God. And there are fully-documented contemporary cases of demon possession that are awesome in scope. And people are not ignorant of this; numerous movies on the subject have had considerable attendance records—movies based on actual cases, *The Entity* and *The Exorcist* being just two.

Some of the documented reports of the phenomenon are even stranger than these movies, as we have been seeing in this book. Cases of wild supernatural activity containing roadsigns that should not be unfamiliar to us.

THE VOICE WIRED TO
THE OTHER SIDE
OF THE UNIVERSE

Within the last ten years, a famous parapsychologist who was psychic realized he was getting far more than he bargained for. The trail of chicken crumbs had been tantalizing, fascinating. The progression of his mind-states, epiphanies of altered consciousness, were chronicles of pre-enlightenment. He was an adept in the wings of Explosion. And then some interesting things began to happen.

One of the most gifted bestselling authors of our day, Malachi Martin, has documented this well-researched case, having met the subject personally, then painstakingly searched the clues of his past. He was also present when the exorcism took place, and knew the exorcist. In his chronicle of five contemporary cases of demon possession (*Hostage to the Devil*, Bantam paperback, 1976), Malachi Martin has named this case, 'The Rooster and the Tortoise'. I myself have been in touch with Malachi Martin from time to time, and he has read and been moved by my own story in India. Though in my case, at the very gates of explosion, I fled.

Yet before that, I remember my own dazzling mind-states of bliss and beyond, as so many do who have had yogic altered states. Eckart Flother, the German correspondent who spent months in India under Rajneesh, reported undeniable Exaltations. Those are the hooks. What boggles the mind is any kind of association these 'good', infinitely desirable blisses could possibly have with the powers of evil—the deceptive powers of evil. It seems inconceivable at first. With inimitable writing, Malachi Martin explores this delicate avenue of consciousness in his chronicles of contemporary possession. It is vital that we have a look (courtesy of Dr Martin).

Of the five cases of possession which he chronicles, perhaps the most flowing documentary of the natural epiphany, the bliss of the high aesthetic in nature, is briefly described in the case of 'Father Bones and Mister Natch'. But the bliss then becomes a kind of telephone receiving station for subtle possessive influences. To get a handle on the dynamics of this mind seduction, we should look at this unitive exaltation with 'Nature'. Then we will get to the remarkable case of the parapsychologist.

Jonathan, the subject, had been in the Canadian wilderness, making lone forays into the forest.

'It was on one of these forays that he found his 'place'—as he called it later. That name, "my place", has now a grisly significance for Jonathan: there his final immersion in demonic possession was accomplished.'

In the early afternoon, he walked along the wilderness river of the region. His whole body and mind suddenly became electrified with a sense of discovery. He stood still.

'That was it. This was the place. Here he would be ordained truly as the priest of the New Being . . . The place was beautiful . . . The center of the riverbed was a soft shifting carpet of sand as white as salt. On each side, like rows of attendant black-cowled monks, there were tiers of boulders and rocks, rounded and smoothed by the overflow of water . . . On each bank there was a small, shelving beach of that pure white carpet of sand sloping up out of the water to a rim of blue and black pebbles, then ferns and grass, then the pines, alders, sycamores, chestnuts. Everything burned in the sun . . .

'Jonathan could see a hundred summer suns mirrored in the green-gray water, and each of them gave off a fire that dazzled him . . . The place was Jonathan's "mirror of eternity", an opening in nature through which he could glimpse the strength of eternity, its softness and cleansing power, and the boundless spaces of its being.'

He fell on his face on the sand as a take-over system guided his body through the rites of a kind of priesthood. He spoke to the surrounding consciousness,

'Make . . . me priest.'

Shiftings in consciousness continued.

'His past was being erased; his entire past . . . all that had entered into the making of what he had been up to that moment, was being flushed from him. He was being emptied of every concept, every logical reasoning, every memory and image which his culture, his religion, his ambient, his reading, had formed in him.'

He waded out into the river for a sort of cosmic baptism.

'Obeying the inner voice, he bent down; his hands groped at the base of a rock and sought to reach to where its roots went deep in water . . . "I was reaching to the veined heart of our world." '

The mystical experience expanded.

'He lost count of ordinary time, of the sun and the wind, of the river and its banks. The wind was a great rushing bird whose wings dovetailed into the green and brown arms of the trees on either side of him. The rocks became living things, his brothers and sisters, his millennial cousins, witnessing his consecration with the reverence that only nature had. And the water around him winked with gleaming eyes as it sang the song it had learned millions of years ago, from the swirling atoms of space, before there was any world and man to hear it. It was an irresistible ecstasy for Jonathan.'

In time Jonathan began to chant to the higher force:

'Lord of Light! Lord of Jesus and of all things! Your slave! Your servant! Your creature! Your priest!'

The voltage of the epiphany increased more in the eye of the hurricane of mystical experience. It drove him beyond his own power. Soon he was zigzagging through the trees 'propelled by the force within him'. Later on he would go through a strange blasphemous ritual and be found by the members of his party, unconscious. After he was exorcised, Jonathan earmarked that occasion as a key turning-point in his possession. His exorcism in the book is a riveting and grotesque experience. And much of what he is led to do in the interim sounds like the path of the average sannyasin under the force of Rajneesh.[1]

The case of 'The Rooster and the Tortoise' goes in depth into the mind seduction of a very bright youth whose epiphanies, rather than entailing a beatific natural revelation, promise a hidden wisdom and psychic power. He surrenders over a period of thirty years to a collective psychic demonic structure known as

The Tortoise, whose approach is the subtle, slow invasion into the mind through a gradual erasure of the sense of good and evil as absolutes. The entity conveys a mystical unifying experience, along with a range of classic yogic *siddhis*.

Carl, the parapsychologist, went to Princeton and Cambridge. He was later to become a recognized authority in the field of parapsychology, until his full possession and exorcism. At that point he dropped out of this dangerous field altogether. He later saw it as an academically acceptable route for promulgating the occult. Like Jonathan, the case cited above, his only escape from desolating annihilation was to turn to Christ. Today he is a healed man.

A key turning-point for Carl was as a teenager. He was standing alone in his father's study in those precious intervening moments before the dinner announcement was made. He was peering into the pages of an encyclopedia when,

'. . . his consciousness underwent a peculiar change. He was not frightened; instead the change put him in what he describes as a great hush. He no longer saw the book in his hand or the shelves of books in front of him . . . His attention was riveted on something else, something totally different from, but in a mysterious way intimate to, all his experience up to that moment in life.

'There was much light, but, he says, a dark light.' Yet that darkness was so brilliant that no detail escaped him. He was not looking at something or at a landscape; he was participating in it, so clear was every detail shown and conveyed to him. What he saw was dimensionless . . . Objects were in that place, but the place was nowhere. And the objects located in that space were not found by coordinates, or seen by the eye, or felt by the hand. He knew them, as it were, by participation in their being. He knew them completely.

'Not only was normal spacial dimension in abeyance as non-extended time. It was not that time seemed to be suspended. There was no time, no duration. He was not looking at the objects for a long or short time . . . there was no sense of duration. It was timeless . . .

'As for a description of that landscape and the objects 'in' it, Carl could only speak vaguely. It was a 'land' . . . a 'region'. It

177

had all you would expect—mountains, sky, fields, crops, trees, rivers. But these lacked what Carl called the 'obscurity' of their counterparts in the physical world. And, although it had no apparent houses or cities, it was 'inhabited'; it was full of an 'inhabiting presence'. There was no sound or echo, but the soundlessness was not a silence, and the echolessness was not an absence of movement. It seemed to Carl for the first time he was freed from the oppression of silence and rid of the nostalgia produced in him by echoes.

'He had a sudden desire, hard to express. A kind of 'show-me' expressed to the presence. Then the whole focus of his vision changed. It was the highlight of his real wonder. He was listening to a small voice and seeing a face he cannot describe. He heard words and saw expressions he cannot put into language. The dominant trait of the voice and face was expressed by him later in the word 'Wait!' He did not know . . . what he was to wait for. But the whole idea was intensely and deeply satisfying. At that point, he was called for dinner and found his return to the world shattering. An immense sadness welled up in Carl at that moment, an indescribable sense of loss.'[2]

He was hooked. And the revelations of *The Tortoise* would progress.

At Princeton, Carl was briefly under the tutelage of a Tibetan mystic in the pursuit of 'higher prayer'. Then he had access to people's thoughts through a clear mind-grid. At about that time he read Aldous Huxley's *The Doors of Perception, Heaven and Hell*, a mescaline-induced account of pantheistic consciousness, and he exulted in it. It was home turf to him. By now he was a professor of parapsychology. Then began his new phase of trances. Through those, his consciousness 'evolved'. One trance was a special breakthrough, when he met his 'friend'.

'When he entered his study from the reception room, his eye fell on the window facing west. The sun had not yet set, but there were incandescent patches and streaks to be seen in the sky. The whole window space looked like a two-panel canvas painted in reds, oranges, blue-grays, gilded whites.

'Carl crossed to the window, and as he gazed at the sunset, there was a gentle but rapid transformation in him. His body became motionless, as if held painlessly immobile by an unseen giant hand. He was frozen, yet without any sensation of cold or paralysis.

'Then the living scene took on the same odd aspect of immobility and frozenness for him. Next, parts of the scene started to disappear.' Things blipped out of view between Carl and the sunset. 'And, of course, the distance between him and the sunset was now a formless vacuum after the disappearance of the objects of his landscape. There was nothing "between" him and the sunset, not even a gap, not even emptiness . . .

'Finally the window itself faded. Carl, meanwhile, had been looking less and less at the colors and hues of the dying sun; and, when the window frame faded, he was "looking merely at the sun", although he cannot express clearly in words the difference between those two sights or the obvious importance it had for him at that moment.'

Carl seemed to shrink in size as the object he was viewing loomed larger and larger. A terror of his awareness disappearing like the foreground seized him. Then his friend appeared. The friend had been there all along.

'No words passed between Carl and his "friend", and no concepts or images that he was aware of. But he knew with absolute certainty he was being "told" that, unless he "nodded" or "gave approval", his progress into nothingness would be a fact.'

Carl thought of challenging this psychic ultimatum but finally acquiesced. He inwardly nodded to the friend.

'Immediately the sense of being reduced to nothingness ceased. Relief flooded his consciousness. Almost simultaneously he heard a voice calling from a great distance.'

It was one of Carl's students coming into the study. Carl soon told the student that he had experienced 'God-manifesting'. His trances soon started to happen before groups of devout students as he became a sort of guru.[3]

Malachi Martin reports, 'In the next eight years Carl experienced an almost permanently altered state of consciousness. He received a similarly permanent perception of what he called the "non-thing" aura (what Huxley had termed the Non-Self aura) surrounding all objects. He had various trances. And above all, he underwent his "exaltation". He was becoming divine, he thought.'

Soon Carl saw things as united. Everything was an aspect of the one being. These were theophanic perceptions. Then 'Carl started to feel some basic differences between what he called "my friend" and this one being, the all-pervasive, free-moving, and independent spirit in which all things were . . .'

This threatened Carl a little. For the next two years he concentrated on astral travel and far-memories of supposedly former lives. Carl soon divided astral travel into three major phases, what he called 'low-gate, mid-gate, and high-gate'. His revelations continued. And this bore concrete results in the experimental lab.

Carl had warned his students that when he reached 'high-gate' his brain-waves would flatten out on the graph. And they did. What worried them more was how Carl's force would dominate them in a sort of umbrella of energy when he returned from trance. And they noticed that he had communications with something else, often by this time. Meanwhile Carl's following of students burgeoned. And he would have trance meetings before large groups. They reported that when the 'presence' appeared, something in them wanted to 'bow' before it. Several students pulled out because they felt the presence was 'unloving' or 'cold' or 'non-human'.

Then it became more and more difficult to retrieve Carl to normal consciousness after these 'spirit-raising sessions'. Now the true signs of possession started to manifest heavily. Meanwhile his control over his followers was becoming ironclad. On one occasion, his return frightened them. Standing up, Carl looked extremely abnormal.

'They became aware that Carl was having difficulties in breathing and standing up straight. He was in a peculiarly bent position. With his soles still flat on the ground and his knees bent, the upper part of his body up to his shoulders was being bent precariously, as if he was falling backward. His chin was sunk in his chest in his effort to straighten up . . . The rule at all sessions had always been clear: no hands on Carl during the session. So nobody moved to help, but everyone watched'.[4]

The devotees were cleared out by Carl's two inner-circle students, and what remained was a twitching oddity with some complex inner battle going on. He was beet-red, in a rage, and muttering cryptic words about the 'Enemy, the Latter' (those in Christ).

Carl took to wearing New-Age neo-pagan emblems, and soon prepared a grand initiatory rite in Greece to be attended by a select few. It was the ancient rite of the Rooster and the Tortoise (Carl's possessing demon masquerading as an ancient oracular deity). The rite itself was something extremely grotesque, with Carl twitching incoherently in the middle of a mosaic floor embodying the ancient religion. Carl was foaming at the mouth, and stuttering a mutation of the name of Christ, which seemed to fill his inner resident with dread.

Soon after that, Carl, or what was left of him, began to send out help signals to those he felt might be able to exorcise him. The eventual exorcism itself brought forth into the room a telekinetic entity that was multiple, calling itself 'The Tortoise'. What ensued was a strange battle. Carl, like many who had become possessed, in some strange way had been 'marked' by his supernatural observers even as a child. They had watched him, and tried to seduce him experientially. That seems to fit the specific ways Sai Baba and Rajneesh were marked as children.

One part of the exorcism went like this:

'We come in the name of the Tortoise. Tortoise. Call us Tortoise. We have the eternity of the Lord of Knowledge.' (Martin describes this voice as similar to that of announcers in the 1930s; affected, openly artificial, always with a note of laughing ridicule.)

'Tortoise, were all of Carl's psychic powers due to your intervention?'

The answer was a confused 'Both . . .' referring to their powers interlayered with his own faculties.

'Let us take his supposed reincarnation, was that your work?'

'We, belonging to the Tortoise, existing in his eternity, have all time in front of us as one unceasing moment . . . Those of the dead who belong to us do our bidding. Everyone in the kingdom does our bidding.'

'And those who don't belong to you?'

'The Latter,' (those in Christ), squeezes out from Carl as a snarl.

181

'The astral travels of Carl? Did you engineer that?'

'Yes.'

'How did you get him into such delusion?'

'Once spirit is confused with psyche, we can let anybody see, hear, touch, taste, know, desire the impossible. He was ours. He is ours. He is of the kingdom.'

Carl is not moving, but his entire body lies once again in the crushed position. The pathos of his captivity makes Hearty (the exorcist) wince. He prays quietly, 'Jesus, give him strength.' Then he tries to continue his interrogation, but the voice interrupts, this time screaming in unbelievable despair.

'We will not be expelled. We have our home in him. He belongs to us.'

'You are the maker of the Non-Self aura?'

'No.'

'How did you use the Non-Self aura in Carl's case?'

'The aura is there for all who can perceive it. Only humans have learned to unsee it. If they saw it continually, they would die.'

'How did you use it?'

'We didn't.'

The aim of the exorcist remains to expose the evil spirits, to make them reveal their own deceptive methods.

'Did Carl see it?'

'Yes.'

'Did you make it clear for him?'

'Yes.'

'Why?'

'He wanted it so.'

'Did he ask you?'

'We offered.'

'Did he know who you were?'

'He knew.'

'Clearly?'

'Clear enough.'

'Did he bilocate?'

'No.'

'What happened?'

'We gave him knowledge of distant places as if he was there.'

182

'Had he a double, a psychic double?'

'We gave him one . . . gave him the knowledge a double would have.'

'When did you start on Carl?'

'In his youth.'

The exorcism is a lengthy, cat-and-mouse affair. Much of it is the surgery of getting the multiple entity to show itself. It is also true to say that, since the demonic creatures are liars, their methods will be a mixture of the truth interlayered with lies. That astral travel is deception in the realm of spiritual bio-mechanics is a truism, but how it works is another matter.

The inquiry continued.

'Where were you leading Carl?'

'To knowledge of the universe.'

'What knowledge?'

'The knowledge that humans are just a part of the universe . . . That they are parts of a greater physical being . . . the universe . . . of matter.'

'And of psychic forces?'

'Yes.'

'And that this was creator of humans?'

'Yes.'

'A personal Creator?'

'No.'

'A psychophysical creator?'

'Yes, indeed, yes.'

'Why did you lead Carl in this way?'

'Because he would lead others.'

'Why lead others in this way?'

'Because then they belong to the kingdom.'

'Why belong to the kingdom?' the exorcist probed.

'Why . . . Why . . . you stand there with your scorched testicles, your smelly clothes, your yellowing teeth, your stinking guts, and you ask why? why? Why? WHY?' It raves. 'Why? Because we hate the Latter (Jesus Christ). We hate. Hate. Hate. Hate. We hate those stained with his blood. We hate and despise those that follow him. We want to divert all from him and we want all in the kingdom where he cannot reach them. Where they cannot go

183

with him. And we want you . . .'

Carl immediately goes ice cold. Thoughts tumble through his mind that the exorcist perceives.

'He is undergoing the feelings and desolation of ideas that beset someone exiled to a baleful land; no warmth, no love, no togetherness, no home, no smile, only the automatic gyrating of controlled beings. Animals frozen by blinding light or tumbling into a private abyss where their free-fall scream never meets its own echo and from which their desires never escape to fulfillment.'

It is a demonic mind-state. Carl seems to say,

'This is my exile from love, my slavery to degrading psychism, and my final tumbling into the aloneness of Hell forever.'[5]

Before the exorcism was complete, Carl had to be willing to let go of the psychic goodies such as astral travel that Tortoise had given him. Martin describes this,

'So desperate was Carl's fear to let go of these privileges and of all his life structure built around them that he cried in pain at the departure even of the purest evil. He screamed in horror as all that he had been convinced was "normal" left him forever . . . because with his will he had chosen to follow the fascinating secrets Tortoise offered to share with him.

'Now, with Tortoise expelled and the truth of Tortoise's identity crystal clear and admitted by him, a frightful disillusionment ran through Carl with the speed of an electric shock, searing and twisting all his thinking and remembering.'[6]

Carl became exorcised when he let go of Tortoise. And in time healed. When he was fit to enter society again, he wrote a letter of apology and repentance to his student following. In the letter he admitted,

'Solemnly and of my own free will, I wish to acknowledge that knowingly and freely I entered into possession by an evil spirit. And, although that spirit came to me under the guise of saving me, perfecting me, helping me to help others, I knew all along it was evil . . . I never enjoyed astral-body-travel, only the illusion of it.'[7]

He confessed that all other psychic gifts were from the same source. In the same letter Carl outlines a facet of his seduction into godhood.

'My central error, which was both intellectual and moral in character, concerned the nature of ordinary human consciousness. Like many before me and many others nowadays, I found that with rigid and expert training I could attain a fascinating state of consciousness: a complete absence of any particular object (in my awareness). I found I could attain a permanency on this plane of consciousness. It finally became a constant environment within me, during my waking hours, no matter what I was doing. It seemed to be pure and therefore sinless, undifferentiated, and therefore universal, simple and therefore without parts—and therefore incorruptible and unchangeable, and therefore eternal.'[8]

When I was in Poona, I was well aware of these modern accounts of exorcism. Among many of the signs I looked for, I watched for these signs on a mass scale, and I saw them. I saw people at varying levels of vulnerability and closeness to possession. Some I am sure bore the marks of possession. I could feel it. Others were well on the path. Rajneesh was in a whole different class of possession: Perfect Possession, that rarefied Satanic initiation that only a Rider of the Cosmic Circuit, an Antichrist, has gone through. It is a state from which there is no turning back, since there is no human remnant left to return to. In this case the demonic power has gone the full distance, so that when the voice speaks and the body moves, in a manner of speaking, it is truly wired to the other side of the universe.

24

AN ENCOUNTER OF THE HIGHEST ORDER OF MAGNITUDE

We had both been waiting three years for this meeting. Now, of all places, it turned out to be in Los Angeles. I was meeting Eckart Flother, the former Swami Anand Virendra, whose remarkable story in Poona had sent shock waves across the community. It was Eckart, a former high-level correspondent, whom CBS' *Sixty Minutes* asked to be the main advisor to their feature show on Rajneesh. He was presently the key advisor to the United States Immigration Department, which was now working overtime in deporting Rajneesh. Eckart knew a lot.

We were in a Los Angeles outdoor cafe, sitting at an open shaded table, away from onlookers. It was a warm January day in 1983. Eckart, who had been with Rajneesh for many months in Poona but who then suddenly fled, was now meeting Sai Baba's one-time top Western disciple, namely me, who had also fled his guru. And John Weldon, a prodigious author and friend, was with us at the table. I had heard about the incredible incident that happened to Eckart in Poona but now I wanted to hear it from him. One thing that had inspired him, after what he had just gone through, was reading about a similar event in *Lord of the Air*, the abridged European version of my book *Avatar of Night*. Our meeting was intense, charged with energy and feeling.

Eckart was recalling a powerful supernatural incident of the highest order of magnitude—an incident that changed him forever. We were taping our conversation, we felt it so important. Eckart at times struggled to put it into English in the precise way it came to him in German.

'It was one of those typically warm, humid Poona nights. I was alone in my hotel room. As you would say, sober as a judge, feeling alert. It was August 1979. It was one of those nights when everything is covered with mosquitoes and nobody can sleep. At any rate I was sitting in my hotel room reading and writing. Perfectly normal. Then all of a sudden, what I saw appearing in my room was incredible! A miracle.

'Let me first say that I was the senior editor of *German Business Week* magazine, and did not have a religious background. And I was used to being objective as a journalist. You need to know that.

'All of a sudden in the left-hand corner of my hotel room I saw a bigger than man-sized, brilliant light. The sheer power, sheer presence was awesome. Rajneesh could not hold a candle to this. I felt instinctively that it was Jesus Christ . . .'

'Had anybody been seeing you who was a Christian?' I asked Eckart. 'Or handing you material on the subject, or anything like that?'

'Absolutely not! At any rate all of a sudden I heard a mighty voice saying to me, "*I want you to become my disciple.*" I was absolutely shaken to bits. I knew right away that this was Jesus calling me. But I did not know what to do with this experience.

'So I returned to the ashram and asked for an appointment with Rajneesh to talk to him. At that time it was not general policy to talk with Rajneesh. Yet I insisted, and that door opened. Well, the evening that I saw him in the smaller group *darshan*—and by the way, here is a picture of it that the ashram photographer took at the exact moment—something very strange happened. At the very moment that I was sitting alone right in front of him, with the group looking on, I felt an evil energy radiating from him as I was sharing this experience. I had an intuitive knowledge that he was not from God. That certainty was complete.

'When I first sat down, Rajneesh was sitting back comfortably in his chair. He was leaning back just looking at me. Then his face shifted. It became irritated, then startled . . . as I shared the visitation. Then when I mentioned that it was Jesus Christ, his face became terrified, he shuddered. His hands got stiff. He became rigid, and began to sit back deep in his chair as though repelled. As though he wanted to thrust his back out through the back of the chair and out of the room.

'At that point I was telling him these words: "I have had a vision. And Jesus Christ appeared and called me. And now Jesus Christ is my Master!" Rajneesh sat for a long time stunned, as though unable to talk. Finally he hissed in a very low voice, sardonically, "Enjoy it." That was it, from then on I was free of him. And I spent the next five weeks on the ashram spying. Seeing people. And that was when I met many of the local Christians. They were staggered by it. Then after five weeks, while I was reading the Bible furiously, and having insight after insight, Jesus Christ spoke to me one more time. He said, "Leave Poona!" And I did immediately. Ultimately I ended up here at Fuller Seminary, Pasadena.'

Eckart's account constituted a modern miracle. It also showed the direct confrontation of powers. This established a base for us to compare notes since both Eckart and I had been heavily into the Eastern Path, had both been under two of the mightiest gurus in the world, and by dramatic miracles had both been set free in similar ways.

I too encountered Christ in an Indian hotel room. It was in Bangalore City the late spring of 1971, before a small group of Westerners who had been under me. All of a sudden, one moment I was in the kingdom of Sai Baba, the next I was in the Kingdom of Christ. With me it was immensely powerful. And my sense of release, joy, was indescribable. Nothing less than a powerful supernatural intervention would have worked with me. After all, it was my guru who had the reputation of being India's biggest miracle worker. As we were discussing this I said to Eckart,

'Well, the world at large can't exactly charge us with being narrow-minded fundamentalists who have never seen the other side, can they?'

'Not at all.'

We were like the man born blind whom Christ instantly healed. When he could see, there was not an argument in the world that could repudiate either the man's testimony, the event, or who was behind it. Now I wanted to get Eckart's view of the manner of creature Rajneesh was.

'In a simple word, Eckart, what is Rajneesh?'

'He is an Antichrist who is demon-possessed. He is not God, that is certain.'

'I want to hear from you any facts that substantiate the evil aspect in operation there. Things you were privy to. Inside stuff. If you will, demonic encounters.'

Eckart, an intelligent German with savvy looks and European charm, and immense likeableness, went deep into his mind. His eyes scanned the slow flow of Santa Monica traffic going down Ocean Boulevard and the beautiful park across the street separating us from the ocean. He was a very youthful, very trim man in his late thirties or early forties. There was an ageless quality about him. Weldon remarked that there was an integrity there. I am not sure I have ever enjoyed a cup of coffee more than that afternoon, listening to Eckart and talking with him. Aside from the fact that this was a three-star cafe-restaurant called Cafe Casino, where the movie set often went and where real European coffee is served.

Eckart covered a fascinating range of details. The common occurrence of various illnesses of specific types amongst the sannyasins. They mirrored Rajneesh's illnesses. Not only venereal disease but allergies, asthmas, intestinal problems of all sorts. That Rajneesh had now discarded Laxmi, his 'number one witch', in favor of Sheela in Oregon. (This was no surprise.) Laxmi was stripped of everything and left behind penniless in India. Meanwhile, in Oregon they had just applied for permission for a crematorium for the ritual of watching the dead being cremated. Eckart personally knew of over 300 cases of sterilization. He mentioned the encounter-group rapes, and enforced sexual switching of partners, including the enforced homosexual option. That their methods of abortion were crude and risky. Then there were the countless suicides and deaths.

'You being a German must have wondered about the death of Prince Welf.'

'Indeed, that was very shrouded. A nurse who was obviously engaged in the situation was saying that Rajneesh was asking her to pull the plug when Prince Welf was under intensive care. And the nurse was supposedly an American. And when *Sixty Minutes* heard of the story—and they got the material basically from me—and Bradley was going to do the interview, at the last

189

minute they could not get the girl to talk. She backed out. Because she was so scared. So very scared. A lot of them who leave are terrified. I know of a girl who was in the inner circle, almost as close as Viveka, and she is really scared. Because she knows things we don't know. She says his real activity is on the spiritual level . . . he vampirizes, assaults people and devours their souls. It is a deep thing.'

'Sai Baba did the same thing, operating on a spiritual plane. Hideous.'

'It is a pattern. I know of some incredible incidents. Let me give you several that come to mind. The first incident involves a fellow who was lying one day on the floor of Buddha Hall meditating. Buddha Hall has a large picture of Rajneesh. All of a sudden Rajneesh came out of the picture, walked over to him, opened his chest, and removed his heart. Rajneesh ate it. He experienced this, it was a frightening experience . . .'

I interrupted, 'You know that in European Satanism they eat the heart.'

'Yeah, and also I think the Incas did it. At any rate, blood was dripping down Rajneesh's beard. And then Rajneesh went back to the picture and spat the heart out. And ever since, the guy felt this was such a spectacular experience, he felt whole. And he said, "And now, everything that I want, I will get." Two days before I met him, he was depressed and did not know what to do with his life. And at this very moment he now felt like nothing could stop him. And the feeling I got at the time, and I was barely a Christian, was that I felt a power in him that was not human.'

'It was a Satanic covenant with Rajneesh,' Weldon interjected.

'Right,' Eckart replied. 'Now the second incident involves a girl I knew. I met her in 1977 at a Christmas party in Berlin. She was a German nurse. Then we met in India. She had been a sannyasin for three years in India. I wasn't a Christian then, and I was in the stage of "hey, what's life all about anyway," and she and I had very good vibes. And after the group we were with, I left my hotel room and she invited me to come in her room to spend the night. And it was like . . . one night all of a sudden she started to tremble and say "I'm so afraid, I'm so afraid". And I said, "What's the matter?" And she said, "I can't talk about it."

'She was in the inner circle or close?' I asked.

'Uh, she was very close, had gone through all the groups. She told me these stories that were amazing. At any rate she said, "One day I was lying in the Buddhafield . . . you know the Buddhafield . . . listening to a tape." And what happened was that she felt that Rajneesh was coming to her spiritually, sexually. And was taking her clothes away, ripping them away, and was making love to her. But she felt that his genital was made out of sheer light, rays of light. And entered her. And it must have been a great experience, but afterwards she felt that he was robbing her of her innocence, life energy. And she said that ever since she has had, off and on, these attacks of fear. And she can't fight it because it is so deep she doesn't know what to do about it.'

Eckart went back to her after he had met Christ.

'One night, after my experience with Jesus, I said, "Why don't you tell me what happened." And then I said, "In Jesus' name, tell me the truth." And she started screaming and yelling. And she was struck on the floor. With all four limbs flailing about. And again I said, "In Jesus' name stop it!" And she stopped and was like a little kid. Crying. It was a real attack. Unfortunately I wasn't educated enough at that time to try an exorcism.'

'One means of possession is through sex,' I interjected.

'Right. Yeah . . . I have come to know that.'

'The accounts in the book *Demonolatry* are about witches locked into inescapable sexual rites with their familiars, demons, with whom they are in covenant. The movie, *The Entity*, is based on this occult phenomenon. The girl is raped by a powerful invisible being of pure evil. Again, the same theme appears in the film *Rosemary's Baby*. It is a world Satanist set-up that only the insiders are aware of. Your standard pragmatist rationalist is totally naive about this stuff. They only wake up, if at all, when they see the damage, after the fact. And they never know why. Human remains have been found all over the Hollywood hills used in Satanic rites. But it makes no sense, and people fail to see the pattern, unless they understand what is at work. There is a network of people right now whose job it is to correlate kids who disappear off the streets, and they number in the thousands, with known Satanic groups. The true facts are grisly indeed.' John and I shared this information with Eckart.

'That's horrible. I have come to see more and more of these

patterns. Well, another case is not unusual but it affected me because the sannyasin was an air hostess, like my former wife, and they were friends. I was married between '68 and '70. I was in Poona in June, seeing her, and she was really in a trance. Her way of talking was "ahh . . . and Rajneesh . . . and Bhagavan . . . and everything is so fine". So I felt really turned off by this sort of talk. "Can't we talk normally?" I asked. I was new to the movement at that time. And so a few weeks later I was again seeing her. And this time she had a very strange smile in which the eyes go somewhere but you really don't know where they are going. And she said, "You know what, next week I will be sterilized. Rajneesh told me so." I asked her why she would do this. And she said, "This is total surrender. And he says we need all the energy for our own growth." I asked her if she was afraid, and she told me "a little bit".

'Now what happened was that they were doing the sterilization in their ashram health clinic. She described that they were pumping up their stomachs. And she was telling me from some experiences that some girls had their colons penetrated by this operation. So the girls were pretty paranoid about this operation. And so I said, "Forget about it." '

'Did any of them die from this?'

'No. But at any rate these experiences in Poona really showed me by the end what was going on there.

'In another case of a friend, the woman wrote to Arup, who was under Laxmi, whether she should have her baby. And Rajneesh wrote her back, "Abort". These were done at a hospital in Poona that was run by a sannyasin. But when she woke up—I was with her at the time—she started screaming. They took out the baby. And she woke up screaming, "Where's my baby?" She cried and cried. She was devastated. I assumed this would end the trip for her. Later she left. I lost track of her, because she went her way. Now she later wrote me a letter shortly before Christmas. And she is now doing seminars in Germany which are dealing with human potential, called Rainbow. And she wrote me in her letter that she's enlightened and whatever she wishes to do she can do! Unbelievable. These people are all of a sudden different. And they cannot leave the track. If they attempt to leave, they fall apart. Those are the fruits that I saw.'

'To read about it and to see it are two things.'

'I did not tell these stories to the TV station because they are not ready to hear it. They don't understand the supernatural. Not really. Especially in Germany.'

Eckart Flother was referring to local stations in Los Angeles. At the time *Stern* magazine of Germany was publishing Eckart's article on Rajneesh. But again, he had to be selective as to what he told them so as not to lose them.

'They just don't have any comprehension of the supernatural.'

Eckart suddenly remembered something with a pained expression. He continued,

'In 1979 an English girl supposedly died from hepatitis—hardly anybody dies from hepatitis—and everybody at the funeral came back with a strange feeling. The girl was lying there on the pyre, before they were going to burn her up then dance and celebrate as they always do. She had this look frozen on her face. The eyes were still open. And she had this expression of *utter fear* . . . and I heard this again and again. People dying on the ashram who all had the same expression in their eyes. As though at the final moment they saw something utterly terrible, unbelievable. Something they must have seen at the very last moment, like Satan appearing. All these people. And I am sure this English girl saw at the last moment what she was into.'

Eckart stopped. Then continued, deliberating. With us he did not have to prove anything. But he reiterated,

'I am a critical journalist. I used to be the senior editor of *German Business Week* and I am used to dealing with facts and real things. I don't come from some emotional spiritual background. So I only believe something when I have seen evidence of it. And my conclusion about these incidents is that it seems to me that with these dying sannyasins, the Satanic reality has been veiled until the moment they died. Then they saw it. It's almost as if they were encountered by it. It could be even that it was a visitation of Satan.'

Eckart thought again.

'Or they were seduced to the point of no return and then he came and claimed them.'

A quiet chill colored our mood as the afternoon progressed. The smell of Poona had become almost tangible to me—that lingering fragrance of death. It was time to pursue a different vein. Eckart remembered an oddity, one of those odd patterns in Poona. At that time he was new to the spiritual realities around him, but he could not deny layer after layer of new experiences that were beyond the natural. Things he had never thought of before or seen before.

'There was one thing which I have not really understood till recently. The time I was in Poona, every night at ten thirty something happened. Every night. For example one night I was sitting in a little fruit stand which had a little German cuckoo clock. At ten thirty it rang thirteen times. Next day it was dinner time (Europeans often eat late) and I was sitting in another place. We heard a noise as if two cars were crashing very loudly, and we ran out of the place and nothing was there.'

'Poltergeist stuff,' Weldon commented.

'Yeah, poltergeist stuff. Another night I was sitting in another restaurant and the waiter came by and threw his tray full of food on our table. Then the next night, in the middle of Poona an elephant walks by.' Eckart was relating this in good humor. 'And I was getting paranoid after some time. I was not so much getting paranoid, I was asking the people around me, "Do you see this?" Or in my hotel, the people next door would be fighting at that hour. All things that are crazy. And the peak event was I was standing there with a couple of people and we were going to cross the street. And there was something, an "Entity", I don't know what it is . . .' he laughed.

'Go on,' I said. (I was looking out for something at this point.)

'It looked like a mixture between you could say—it has the size of a big truck but with a lot of lights. So it was like . . . and this came down with high speed, I would say in German terms it was two hundred kilometers per hour, which is about one hundred and twenty miles per hour. High speed. You could also say it looked a little bit like a dragon. And this entity mixture between whatever came down the road like . . . whhhhshhhh . . . and I was standing there . . .'

I had to ask just to make sure, 'Were you stoned at the time?'

'No, I was straight,' Eckart replied in earnest. 'I was stoned occasionally, but in all these major ones I was straight.'

'When you say "Entity", it was alive?' John and I asked.

'But I mean this size. It was very tangible and in the first place the image was like an old locomotive, chugging, but the interesting thing was a lot of light all over it.'

'You never find anything on an Indian street going two hundred kilometers an hour. That's an impossibility.' My years in India were surfacing.

'And you see the interesting thing was it was like . . . normally Indian roads are full of people, stuff like this, and this street was empty, perfect set-up.'

'What was the feeling you had when it went by?'

'It was a mixture of entertainment and being a bit frightened. I said, "Oh my goodness". Because I couldn't see it properly. But nothing flies down a narrow Indian road at two hundred kilometers an hour. It is physically impossible. This was very tangible. So I had the feeling that something was going on, especially the Poona ashram.'

'It's an evil city,' I said. 'A lot of these gods in temples actually look like locomotives. I remember the huge Kali form in the temple in Calcutta . . . looked just like a locomotive. And the Bible speaks of the forms that idols are based on as being elemental spirits that are demonic.'

Certainly what Eckart had seen fitted the pattern. I was convinced, with Eckart and John, that it was a rare demonic manifestation. It sounded like a massive collective entity. For the genealogy of many of India's gods went back to Babylon, the accursed civilization that Cyrus the Mede hammered into the ground. Like 'Pazzuzzu', the Babylonian god in *The Exorcist*, the ancient gods were mirrored embodiments of demonic forces. Village Indians encountered these gods all the time in visions. And what they were guided to do often involved, according to record, human sacrifices and other activities that were evil.

'Indeed, you were at the hub of a black energy field,' I said.

Eckart then concluded,

'I know today that it was some sort of demonic force.'

The tone became extremely solemn all of a sudden. A sadness filled Eckart's face. He brought out a black book, a diary. It had a sad story behind it. He slid it across the table. It was an ashram diary with printed teachings of Rajneesh and spaces on each page for daily notes. On the first page was the name 'Deva Rupen'. Below was the anglicized 'Ron Rickards'.

'He's dead now. He gave it to me not long before he died. He was on a diet of milk and opium. He was one of Rajneesh's first close disciples, meeting Rajneesh in Northern India and financing him—you see he was an Australian multi-millionaire. Soon after I had come to Christ, my girlfriend and I saw him collapse, faint, in the ashram, and we carried him off to a hospital. It was then that he said, "One day you will need this . . . use this book. Please have it." He was on a downward course of disintegration and could not escape. I tell you, I would like to do a film of this book.'

It was the common story of someone being used, sucked dry, then being left in the road as people with more goods arrived. Eckart was given the diary the day before he left Poona on the plane. It was on the plane that he opened the book and felt his heart sink. Then Jane Dingle wrote Eckart that Rupen had jumped out of a window in a suicide attempt. They flew the crippled survivor back to Australia but to no avail. His suicide attempt had worked.

'Just recently, when I loaned this book to Channel Four here in Los Angeles,' Eckart told us, 'they were so moved they showed some pages on TV.

'This diary is an eye-opener. You can see him daily, how do you say, deteriorating. Fighting for his life. Right there watching himself deteriorate and writing it down. This in itself is a document that is unbelievable.'

I reached out and grasped the black book. John and I would only keep the diary until the next day. Then we would return it to Eckart in his Santa Monica apartment. It was an infinitely sad chronicle of somebody trapped. A study of death—of someone going the limit, breaking endless boundaries, and still being empty, unfulfilled. And alone, that cosmic loneliness that so many of them felt.

Weldon and I xeroxed the diary and contemplated it at a house in Thousand Oaks where friends let us stay. Somehow I felt, along with Eckart, that we had been spared, we had escaped our Indian experience alive. Not just alive, but meeting, incredibly, with Jesus Christ. It was too much.

'Tell me some of the things in there that made your hair stand on end,' I asked.

'It is very difficult, because he is using so many different ways of writing. You see that he is totally fragmented. He does not know where to go. He is experimenting with all kinds of drugs. He feels death is coming . . . death is coming. He can't stop it.'

That night I felt the tragic spell within the black diary. Most of the pages in the black book had massive lettering, squiggles, cryptic anagrams, weird cartoons, and private notes. Accounts of coming and going to Goa, Bombay, then relationships with this girl and that. The void of emptiness within. Accounts of this drug and that drug. And a soul dying inside. His address was like Eckart's, The Mobos Hotel at Bund Garden Road, Poona.

I will record a sample page that illustrates Deva Rupen's wide mood swings.

Monday 15 January. 'Feels wonderful to be alive. To breathe. To be in a magical land. Feel like I've always been here. India is pure reality.'

But the next day, Tuesday, things had changed:

'Feel so lonely . . . cry, cry, I am crying, so very lonely among all these so called sannyasins, so lonely, very. Who are my friends? What? Why? How? No! No! . . . Is there anything worthwhile? Feel pain now today. Cry. Yell. Reminisce. The past was beautiful. Now I am lost in India. Why the f . . . am I here??'

On to Wednesday and it would be a recurrent message:

'Felt a little suicidal today. Mahavir said, "The only valid way to suicide is to stop breathing, stop eating, stop drinking, stop moving—and die." Pretty weird I feel.'

On parting Eckart and I felt infinitely grateful that we had escaped India alive, by the skin of our teeth. But many didn't. They were either flown out in body bags, or buried somewhere in the infinitely dense sub-continent. But perhaps nothing less, we concluded, could have driven us to the Kingdom of Christ. We had exhausted many of the world's alternatives, from atheism to pantheism. But truly, it had taken a miracle to reach us. So too with John Weldon. Though he did not share our Indian experience, he had in his own way flown with the spirit of the age.

Reading the diary that night reinforced our gratitude for a

sovereign God of infinite good, and not the god of the gurus. This was the diary of a madman whose god smelled again and again like Satan as he disemboweled the live Ron Rickards, also known as Deva Rupen—who is now dead. You could say this part is in honor of him—and that fragile moment when he passed on his diary to Eckart.

'You will need this,' he said.

UNMASKING THE
HORNED GOD

It was a sunny Saturday morning. We were on Eckart's cosy terrace in Santa Monica. The previous night in Thousand Oaks with Deva Rupen's diary had been macabre. Reading page after page from a man chained to his own death and watching it. There was a pornographic quality about it. Now we were going deep into what we knew. Finding common patterns.

But first Eckart had a bit of news. Eckart had just heard that one of Rajneesh's top disciples had defected from the movement. It was the highly visible bodyguard, Shiva Murthi, who had been with Rajneesh for years. Now he was back in Scotland. What triggered the defection was what happened when he and a friend were canoeing; the friend got swept off in the rapids and started drowning. When Shiva Murthi phoned Sheela for a helicopter, she brusquely told him to forget the friend. That broke something in him and he left Oregon. Now in Scotland he was beginning to wake up out of his daze.

Shiva Murthi (meaning 'the embodiment of Shiva') had written to *Stern* magazine following Eckart's recent article saying,

'Rajneesh Mohan is directing an unscrupulous, international, multi-million-dollar enterprise. Individuals and groups that are in his way are fought by inhuman means . . . His vision of the world consists of the view that only he and his followers are the heirs of the earth. Does this sound familiar?'

He called it a community of betrayal and hypocrisy.

Eckart tied in another pattern. I knew of it from a separate source—a woman with whom I had spoken on the phone, and who had been in Vienna in the mid-seventies. She had heard from a sannyasin that Rajneesh had been discussing the efficacy of using gas as an ultimate means to bring about a phenomenon known as orgasmic-death. That too had an uncomfortably familiar feeling. He could have a mass-death enlightenment. At that time, our informant remembered, a number of highly appointed German sannyasins were in Germany trying to recapture Hitler's obsessive occult prize, 'the spear of destiny'. With that in possession, it is said, a sorcerer can gain control of the world—an interesting obsession for an Indian guru. (Our witness friend was at the ZIST community in Bavaria, which became a center for sending Germans to India.)

John Weldon could not resist opening the dark leather book in front of him and reading a passage several thousand years old:

'Woe to those who drag iniquity with the cords of falsehood, and sin as if with cart ropes. Woe to those who call evil good, and good evil; who substitute darkness for light and light for darkness; who substitute bitter for sweet, and sweet for bitter' (Isaiah 5:18-19).

This was rather reassuring in a topsy-turvy world of values, or non-values, especially in contrast to the other black book, Deva Rupen's diary which showed the blight of a soul withered and robbed of its essence where evil and good had been homogenized into one substance.

Were we finding simply a mad random pattern, or was there a deeper pattern to it? These odd details surrounding Rajneesh and other groups spanning history, did they confirm that we were up against the Kingdom of Darkness by its ancient odor? There were recurrent themes. In England of antiquity, the horned god would sit and watch the Druid orgies. He was an embodiment of the Evil One. On his throne he would oversee the sexual orgies, the dancing women. The energy level would be raised at the moment of a human sacrifice. Reports of the same activities appear today on police records from Hampshire, England to Los Angeles. We could picture Rajneesh, his swaying women, *shaktis*, his overseeing orgies, his confusing good and evil . . . Then there were the victims.

The other book
How do you explain enlightenment? Enlightenment is the ultimate initiatory giving over of the identity—the mind, spirit, and soul—to another power to become the occupant. It is a self-

annihilating surrender. The new occupant is no longer human. It is operating on a superhuman level of intelligence. And it has strategy, deception, and power—this is the timeless theme. That final rite of surrender has a recurrent configuration before the cosmic possession becomes irreversible.

What manner of high cosmic intelligence? It is mentioned: 'Ye wrestle not against flesh and blood, beloved, but dominions, powers, principalities, wickedness in high places' (Ephesians 6:12). Wicked principalities. Wicked powers. It was all there in that other black book.

And ones like Rajneesh or Sai Baba, is there a category for them? Yes, they show up in the ancient epistle written to the Thessalonian church. They were foretold by the Apostle Paul speaking as the mouthpiece of the Holy Spirit:

'And the man of lawlessness is revealed, the son of perdition, who opposes and exalts himself above every so-called god or object of worship, so that he takes his seat in the temple of God, displaying himself as being God . . . that is the one whose coming is in accord with the activity of Satan, with all power and signs and false wonders and with all the deception of wickedness for those who perish, because they did not receive the love of the truth so as to be saved . . .' (2 Thessalonians 2:3-10).

This passage deals with the Man of Sin, the tradition of the Antichrists who claim to be God. And the battle is for each human soul. A soul can be purchased for as little as a meal. Consider Esau selling himself for a meal, people auctioning themselves off in despair to the lowest bidder. The kingdom of The Tortoise gathered victims into its demonic eternity as it did with the famous parapsychologist, Carl. Had Carl not panicked, The Tortoise would have succeeded. Then the parapsychologist would have become 'enlightened', and entered the ranks of the gurus. He would have been some kind of Rider, though only if his initiation was of a certain level.

What happens within the surrendering vehicle? The total desecration, degradation, defamation of a soul during the ritual. That is the recurrent theme. Ecstasies may appear, but the rites have a certain definite pattern.

For years I had studied North Indian Tantra and seen that it was the original model of European Satanism. The Ancient One

201

had left his smell and trail of blood across the centuries, from Nimrod of Babylon, to the horned god of the Druids, flickering hither and yon in a wild energy pattern. But the Tantrics had it down. Surrender by degradation—eating feces, coitus with dead bodies, cannibalism, human sacrifice—remember 'blowing the roof off of conventional morality'—orgies, worship of Shiva . . . Siva . . . Satan, The Ancient One. Shiva with his cobras and trident. Are we getting a cosmic entity who keeps stepping into the historical picture? And only one other black book warns about this pattern, the Bible.

Why is man degraded? If man is made 'in the image of God', that likeness has to be once and for all smeared and defaced beyond recognition as an act of surrender on the part of the man and as an act of cosmic blasphemy by The Evil One. That is part of the ancient pattern.

How are we in God's image? We have intelligence, will, emotions, personality, a conscience, a sense of good and evil. And what is systematically destroyed by Rajneesh, Sai Baba, the other Riders of the Cosmic Circuit? The mind, the ego, the will which is surrendered, the conscience, the sense of good and evil. But this rite can only be made consummate by an ultimate ritual. That is where the inner layers of the onion begin. One is seduced by high-sounding pantheistic philosophy until then, then he bows at the dark altar of the demon god, he kills or he eats feces, or he surrenders to the energy of an orgy . . . and his dissolution is in effect. Then it is only a matter of time till full possession takes place.

What is the carrot held out on the end of the stick? Nothing new to be sure. The promise of one's becoming God, or a god, or a goddess. And the reward of Knowledge, and the transcendence of death, and some kind of ecstasy.

And where did this configuration first enter into human history? The third chapter of Genesis, in the Garden of Eden. Eve was promised Godhood, immortality, and knowledge for a conscious willful act against her God. The creature desired to become God. Hence her first act. Is it an ancient theme? It could not possibly reach further back into antiquity. And it is coming into the full light of day in our generation. So it seemed to us.

And in all the yogas, all the mysticisms, all of the mystery

religions going down the ages, knowledge was a strong entice-
ment. But the ultimate reward was Godhood. That was the 'con'
that The Tortoise first got Carl with—Knowledge. Such is the
thousand-petaled lotus that I once sought through yoga under
Baba, and millions and millions of yogis have tried to attain it.

At times, Rajneesh has been brazenly revealing from his
throne. The bearded Godman would leak out such revelations
as, 'God has to take the help of the Devil to run the affairs of the
world. Without the Devil, even he cannot run the affairs. So I
had to choose devils, Beelzebubs, so then I thought why not with
style? Why not with taste? Devils there are going to be. I decided
for women, more are wanted. Also, my ashram makes no
difference between the Devil and Divine. I absorb all. So whoever you are, I am ready to absorb you. And I use all sorts of
energies . . . the devilish energy can be used in a divine way . . .
And this is only a beginning. When more devils come, you will
see.'[1]

Doubtless the crowd surrounding Rajneesh's throne would
nod with amusement, delighting in his abandon, his cleverness if
you will. But did he have the last laugh, charming them all the
way to hell? How could it be any other way.

Beyond degrading man in the image of God, other themes are
recurrent, with Rajneesh, with Tantra, with Satanism, with
certain forms of Witchcraft, with the ancient Druids, and with
countless other groups bearing the same mark. Whatever crawled
inside Rajneesh Chandra Mohan at the age of twenty-one, at
Explosion, knew the deep mysteries of its god. Like The
Tortoise, it had the plan of the ages in its own eternity, which was
linked in the demonic hierarchy of hosts, multiple entities as
timeless as the void, to the arch demon of them all in cosmic high
command—Satan himself.

These cosmic powers of evil had their falling-out with God
eons ago, according to the Bible. They had been incredibly
powerful, supernatural creatures of a wide variety—angels. But
something happened in the crusts of time by their act of will.
Their intelligence and will became bent. Now they were the
wicked Potentates who, like The Tortoise, hated 'The Latter'.
They could crawl deep into the body of Rajneesh Chandra
Mohan, Sai Baba, or Carl . . . but only under certain laws of will,

of surrender. And their eye has been on others. They have doubtless been waiting for a long time for Ram Dass to let down his guard. And they were waiting in the wings to jump inside of me and Eckart; this I knew. There was a pattern to the prying open of the victim, the pre-possessed.

What emerged in the Charles Manson case was that when the level of fear in the victims was raised to a peak, another energy-presence became operative in the field. The Encounter groups on the ashram raised the energy field by shock and 'blowing the lid off'. Weldon read from a book on witchcraft, 'The object of ritual, including the Black Mass, is to raise power to implement and strengthen the mental force of its practitioners . . . there is no doubt that the emotions generated by the Black Mass constitute a considerable energy potential.'[2]

And death or killing? Wouldn't that raise the temperature of the ritual?

Human sacrifice

We had another book, *The Black Arts*, whichWeldon cited:
'In the later grimoires the sacrifice is done . . . to increase the supply of force in the circle. In occult theory a living creature is a storehouse of energy, and when it is killed most of this energy is suddenly liberated . . . The amount of energy let loose when the victim is killed is very great, out of all proportion to the animal's (or victim's) size or strength.'[3]

The same book continues this theme:
'The spirit or force which is summoned in the ceremony is normally invisible. It can appear visibly to the magician (occultist, yogi, witch, Satanist) by fastening on a source of energy on the physical plane of existence. It may do this by taking possession of one of the human beings involved in the ritual.'[4]

The height of the emotions, and the sacrifice, serve to up the ante. To Eckart, this started to mirror what he had been feeling and saying. Weldon read on:
'The most important reason for the sacrifice, however, is the . . . charge which the magician obtains from it . . . It would obviously be more effective to sacrifice a human being because of the far greater psychological 'kick' involved. Eliphas Levi said that when the grimoires talk about killing a kid they really mean a

human child . . . there is a tradition that the most effective sacrifice to demons is the murder of a human being.'[5]

Rajneesh's death-orgasm surfaces in Satanism and Tantra.

'If this (sacrifice) is combined with the release of sexual energy in orgasm, the effect is to heighten the magician's frenzy and the supply of force in the circle still further. This is the other "sacrifice" which Crowley (the Satanist) and other modern magicians skirt mysteriously around—"with regard to which the Adepts have always maintained the most profound secrecy" and which is the "supreme mystery of practical Magick." '[6]

Death, orgasm, sacrifice, energy, power, entity-presence, possession—the ancient chemistry. I could picture Teertha in the encounter group playing with the elements of this ancient knowledge and raising the energy stakes with rapes, mind-shocks, and violence by 'blowing the lid off'. The natural progression was to kill somebody in a ritual orgy. But when would he reach this point? Or had he in secret already done so? I could imagine it in Poona at night—Teertha, with his horned god on the throne, Rajneesh, looking on in a charged atmosphere of dancing women, whose role was identical to the ancient witch. Helping to provide *shakti*, energy to the ritual. We could only speculate. It might explain the countless disappearances in Poona. All an accidental pattern? Maybe, but not likely. Not according to that frightened psychiatrist who was under the death threat in Poona.

Mircea Eliade, in probing into the history of witchcraft, said,

'All features associated with European witches are . . . claimed also by Indo-Tibetan yogis and magicians.' And, along with a range of occult powers common to both, the Indians 'boast that they break all the religious taboos and social rules: that they practice human sacrifice, cannibalism, and all manner of orgies, including incestuous intercourse, and that they eat excrement, nauseating animals, and devour human corpses. In other words, they proudly claim all the crimes and horrible ceremonies cited *ad nauseam* in the Western European witch trials.'[7]

It was hardly new in India. In Assam, a Tantric haven over the long centuries, the temple of Kamakhya (Durga) was famous for human sacrifices. In the 1500s they had 140 people beheaded at a single mass sacrifice. The members of that group, the Aghoris, were famous for their cruelties and their orgies. There, subjects volunteered to be sacrificed to the goddess Kali. Their freedom was a total anarchy. They worshipped Shiva and Kali.[8]

The Aghoris ate from human skulls, haunted ceremonies, and practiced cannibalism, up until and including this century.

'Crooke cites the case of an Aghori from Ujjain who, in 1887, ate a corpse from the pile at the burning ghat. The justification is also not new. "There is neither good nor evil, pleasant nor unpleasant." '[9]

Blowing the lid off taboos was an art, and there are only so many routes available to go the limit. The ancients knew that. Again, that same pattern.

Meanwhile the Chingons in the Santa Ana Mountains above Los Angeles had begun this branch of the ancient path, eating the living hearts of sacrificed animals. And several groups in the Topanga Canyons of the Hollywood Hills were combining Black Magic, drugs, orgies, and sacrifice. (The Mutilation Research Center)

But as Rajneesh would say, it all depends on how you do it, what state of mind the act is committed in. That too was not new. The *Vajrayana Tantra* cited the common teaching,

'By the same acts that cause some men to burn in hell for thousands of years, the yogi gains his eternal salvation.'

On the subject of death-energy Rajneesh has said,

'But the greatest blessing is to be present when a Buddha dies. You can simply ride on that energy. You can simply take a quantum leap with that energy . . . It is going to happen to many of my sannyasins. The day I will disappear, many of you are going to disappear with me.'[10]

The liberation of energy at death, an old occult theme, was an early obsession with Rajneesh who as a youth was cloying around funeral ghats in Maharashtra.

We considered the horned god. Its roots went way back:

'This symbol of the horned head with a torch between the horns is much much older than the time of Abu-el-Atahiyya. It can be traced back to ancient India . . . (Then) at Mendes (the Goat of Mendes) an actual sacred ram was adored with strange rites described by Herodotus.'[11]

We also noticed that Allen Edwards, in *The Jewel and The Lotus*, has given an extraordinary insight into Tantric Eastern

Yoga. He shows that its orgies are identical to the way in which medieval witches are said to have regarded their Devil, the 'Man in Black', when he presided over the coven wearing his ritual grand array, the Satan-head, horned mask. A number of lesser Tantric Indian gurus watched and coached the sexual unions of their following. I had known a New York couple twelve years back who were both driven insane by something the guru did when he oversaw them. He was now in New York, furthering his ring of adherents, this minor guru. The New Age was very into the idea of initiation, but milder, sweeter, more aromatic ones. The vicious and obvious path of Rajneesh and the Tantrics was a far more radical initiation than most New Agers would ever consider. That was too blatantly 'evil' to most people. The majority needed a far more gradual incline. The implications of 'there is neither good nor evil', driving them the route of experimentally 'blowing the roof off', on the fast-track of 'Explosive' techniques, that comes in way down the path.

Some inner-ring New Agers have spoken about a Luciferic Initiation. But this is not new either. What was it? A letter a hundred years old in the British Museum mentioned the plan: a global Luciferic initiation. Albert Pike, Grand Mason of the Lodge of the Scottish Rite of Freemasonry in Charleston, South Carolina had written a letter to Mazzini. The plan was to tamper with world consciousness, to manipulate the finances to create a one-world order, to bring in a series of Messiahs, to have three world wars, of which the third would disillusion humanity with both atheistic humanism (communism) and Judeo-Christianity. (The letter was dated 15 August 1871, and until recently was on display at the British Museum Library in London.) But there was more.

By the Albert Pike plan, the stage would be set for a world messiah and his Luciferic initiation to begin the dawn of the light of Lucifer in the New Age. Again, Pike's proposal was one among many recurrent themes.

Meanwhile in the Spring of 1982, an ad in the *New York Times* announced the advent of Maitreya, the world Messiah, perhaps just another prototype in the wings. This ad was paid for by the Lucis Trust (formerly the Lucifer Publishing Company). And at around the same time Rajneesh was appearing weekly in *Time* and *Newsweek* magazines in prominent ads. Were all these gurus linked together? Not necessarily at all. But a blueprint seemed to be perceptible. And who could possibly tell how many minions had been marshalled, separately, unknowingly, to form the grand matrix, if biblical revelation on the subject was correct about 'a pattern'.

But whether Pike and others were vehicles for the secret plan or not, the two-thousand-year-old Book of Revelation already had the master-plan for a world order with Satan incarnate at the helm as the Antichrist. His level of explosion, you could say, was the most total, and his occupant the most powerful and earth-shaking.

Were we overstating the power of these movements? Eckart had been amazed that a whole nation had become seduced in Hitler's Germany. But that was when he was a correspondent, before he fell under the spell of Rajneesh and saw so many liberated, intelligent, high-minded, talented people utterly seduced by something diabolical. And he of all people had been one of them! So too with me when I was in South India under Sai Baba. Eckart would say, 'Hitler took a whole nation.'

Only an encounter of the highest order of magnitude in the bowels of India could rescue Eckart and me, and we could say truly, 'In Christ there is no East nor West.' Hope was something that we thought we could never find. Until the Alpha and Omega himself entered from deep heaven in our souls and invaded the Kingdom of Darkness. Meanwhile, as far as we were concerned, the horned god had been unmasked forever as his footprints became more and more evident trailing across the world and across the ages.

For more detailed study

BHAGWAN SHREE RAJNEESH

Books by Rajneesh himself:

The Book of the Secrets, I, Harper & Row, San Francisco, 1974
Dimensions Beyond the Known, Wisdom Garden, Los Angeles, 1975
The Mustard Seed, Harper & Row, San Francisco, 1975
The Psychology of the Esoteric, Harper & Row, San Francisco, 1977
The Mystic Experience, Motilal Banarsidass, New Delhi, 1977
Meditation: The Act of Ecstasy, Perennial Library, San Francisco, 1978
I Am the Gate, Perennial Library, San Francisco, 1978

Books about Rajneesh:

Yarti, Swami Anand, *The Sound of Running Water, a photo-biography of Bhagwan Shree Rajneesh and his work, 1974-78*, Poona Rajneesh Foundation, 1980
Joshi, Vasant, *The Awakened One: the life and work of Bhagwan Shree Rajneesh*, Harper & Row, San Francisco, 1982
Bharti, Ma Satya, *Death Comes Dancing*, Routledge & Kegan Paul, London, 1981
Bharti, Ma Satya, *Drunk on the Divine*, Grove Press, New York, 1981
Paper by Eckart Flother, later published as *Rajneesh*, IVP Booklet

Also important is *Sannyas* magazine, 1978-81

211

SAI BABA

Books by Sai Baba himself:

Bhagavatha Vahini, Sri Sathya Sai Publication and Education
Foundation, Bangalore and Bombay
Sathya Sai Speaks, *Volumes 1-9*, Sri Sathya Sai Foundation,
Vol. 1 1970
Summer Showers in Brindavan 1972, Sri Sathya Sai Foundation
Upanishad Vahini, Sri Sathya Sai Foundation, second edition
1970
Truth—What is Truth? Volume 1, Gulab Bhawan, New Delhi,
1975

Books about Sai Baba:

Brooke, Robert Taliaferro, *Avatar of Night*, Vikas, Ghaziabad,
U.P., 1982
Kasturi, N, *Sathyam—Shivam—Sundaram: The Life of
Bhagavan Sri Sathya Sai Baba*, Parts 1-3, Sri Sathya Sai
Foundation, 1971, 1972, 1973
Kasturi, N, *The Life of Bhagavan Sri Sathya Sai Baba*, Dolton,
Bombay, 1969
Howard, Murphet, *Sai Baba, Man of Miracles*, Samuel Weiser,
New York, 1976
Sandweiss, Samuel H, *Sai Baba the Holy Man*, Birt Day, San
Diego, 1975

Also important is *Yoga Journal*, 'India: Land of Timeless Flow',
May-June 1977

MUKTANANDA

Books by Swami Muktananda himself:

Mukteshwari, Part 2, Shree Gurudev Ashram, Ganeshpuri, 1973
Play of Consciousness, Harper & Row, San Francisco, 1974
Getting Rid of What You Haven't Got, Word, Santa Fe, 1974
Swami Muktananda American Tour 1970, Shree Gurudev
Siddha Yoga Ashram, Piedmont, 1974
Siddha Meditation: *Commentaries on the Shiva Sutras and other sacred texts*, SYDA Foundation, Oakland, 1975
Where Are You Going? SYDA Foundation, South Fallsburg,
New York, 1982
Muktananda: *Selected Essays* (ed. Paul Zweig), Harper & Row,
1976

RAM DASS

Books by Ram Dass:

Be Here Now, Crown, New York, 1971
The Only Dance There Is, Doubleday, New York, 1973
Journey of Awakening: *A Meditator's Guidebook*, Bantam, New York, 1978
Grist for the Mill, Bantam, New York, 1979

Other Books on Eastern Religion and Witchcraft

Adler, Margot, *Drawing Down the Moon: Witches, Druids, Goddess-Worshippers and Other Pagans in America Today*, Viking, New York 1979

Cavendish, Richard, *The Black Arts*, Putnams, New York, 1967

Eliade, Mircea, *The Sacred and the Profane: The Nature of Religion*, Harvest, New York, 1959

Eliade, Mircea, *Patterns in Comparative Religion*, Meridian, Cleveland, 1963

Eliade, Mircea, *Yoga, Immortality and Freedom*, Princeton University, 1973

Eliade, Mircea, *Occultism, Witchcraft and Cultural Fashions*, University of Chicago, 1976

Glass, Justine, *Witchcraft: the Sixth Sense*, Wilshire, Hollywood, 1974

Mehta, Gita, *Karma Cola: Marketing the Mystic East*, Simon & Schuster, New York, 1979

Moody, Edward J., 'Magical Therapy: an anthropological investigation of contemporary satanism' in Irving Zaretsky and Mark Leone (eds) *Religious Movements in Contemporary America*, Princeton University, 1974

Thomas, P., *Hindu Religion, Customs and Manners*, D.B. Taraporevala Sons, Bombay, fourth edition

Valiente, Doreen, *An ABC of Witchcraft, Past and Present*, St Martin's Press, New York, 1973

FOOTNOTES

Chapter 1

1. N. Kasturi, *Sathyam-Shwam-Sundaram Part II: The Life of Bhagwan Sri Sathya Sai Baba*, Bangalore, India, n.d., p. 79

Chapter 4

1. Swami Muktananda, *Play of Consciousness*, Harper & Row, 1978, p. 65
2. ibid, p. 66
3. ibid, pp. 75–78
4. ibid, p. 81
5. ibid. pp. 84–85
6. Paul Zweig, *Muktananda: Selected Essays*, Harper & Row, 1976, pp. 99–100
7. Muktananda, *Play of Consciousness*, op. cit., pp. 87–88
8. ibid, p. 88–89
9. ibid, p. 103–104
10. ibid, pp. 104–105
11. ibid, p. 105
12. ibid, p. 106
13. ibid, p. 175
14. ibid, pp. 182–84

Chapter 8

1. Ram Dass, *Grist for the Mill*, Bantam, 1979, p. 63

Chapter 9

1. *Yoga Journal*, April 1979

Chapter 13
1. *Sannyas Magazine*, July-Aug 1978, p. 33

Chapter 14
1. *Sannyas*, July-Aug 1980, p. 19
2. See also *The Mustard Seed*, 1975, pp. 292–93
3. *Sannyas*, July-Aug 1980, p. 3
4. *Sannyas*, March-April 1976, p. 13
5. Vincent Bugliosi, KABC-TV, Feb 16 1976
6. *Sannyas*, Jan-Feb 1978, p. 5
7. *Sannyas*, Sept-Oct 1979, p. 26
8. *Los Angeles Times*, 10 Jan 1981

Chapter 15
1. Vasant Joshi, *The Awakened One: The Life and Work of Bhagwan Shree Rajneesh*, p. 23
2. Rajneesh, *Dimensions Beyond the Known*, p. 153
3. ibid, p. 158
4. ibid, p. 156
5. Swami Anand Yarti, *The Sound of Running Water, A photobiography of Bhagwan Shree Rajneesh and his work 1974–1978*, Poona Rajneesh Foundation, 1980, p. 15. See also Rajneesh, *Dimensions Beyond the Known*, pp. 158–80
6. ibid
7. *The Sound of Running Water*, p. 15; cf. Vasant Joshi, *The Awakened One*, pp. 30–40
8. Yarti, *The Sound of Running Water*, p. 14
9. Joshi op. cit., p. 39
10. ibid
11. ibid, p. 40
12. ibid, p. 34
13. ibid, p. 31
14. ibid
15. ibid, p. 41
16. ibid, p. 48; cf. pp. 35–40
17. ibid, p. 51; cf. *Dimensions Beyond the Known*, p. 160, 'In one respect I was as good as mad'
18. Rajneesh, *Dimensions Beyond the Known*, p. 160
19. ibid

20. Rajneesh, *Tao: The Pathless Path*, Vol. 2, Poona: Rajneesh Foundation, 1979, pp. 296–97

Chapter 16
1. Rajneesh, *Tao: The Pathless Path*, op. cit., Vol. 2, p. 297
2. Yarti, *The Sound of Running Water*, op. cit., pp. 26–27
3. ibid
4. ibid
5. Rajneesh, *Dimensions Beyond the Known*, p. 161
6. Rajneesh, *The Discipline of Transcendence; Discourses on the Forty-Two Sutras of Buddha* Vol. 2, Poona: Rajneesh Foundation, 1978, pp. 301–310
7. Yarti, *The Sound of Running Water*, op. cit. p. 29

Chapter 17
1. Yarti, *The Sound of Running Water*, p. 29
2. Rajneesh, *The Discipline of Transcendence*, op. cit. Vol. 2, pp. 313–314
3. ibid, p. 314

Chapter 18
1. *Sannyas*, Jan-Feb 1978, pp. 11–15
2. Ma Bharti, *Drunk on the Divine*, Grove Press, 1980, p. 147
3. *Sannyas*, Jan-Feb 1978, pp. 11–15
4. *Sannyas*, Sept-Oct 1978, p. 23
5. *Sannyas*, May-June 1978, p. 11
6. ibid

Chapter 19
1. Gita Mehta, *Karma Cola*, Simon & Schuster, 1979, p. 30
2. *Sannyas*, March-April 1978, p. 12
3. Rajneesh, *I Am the Gate*, Perennial Library, 1978, p. 180
4. ibid, p. 165
5. Rajneesh, *Dimensions Beyond the Known*, Wisdom Garden Books, 1975, pp. 135–137
6. Yarti, *The Sound of Running Water*, op. cit. p. 153

7. ibid, p. 68
8. Ma Bharti, *Drunk on the Divine*, Grove Press, 1980, pp. 53–54
9. *Sannyas*, Sept-Oct 1979, p. 41
10. ibid, p. 31

Chapter 20

1. *Sannyas*, July-Aug 1978, p. 34
2. From a copy of the original letter also printed in *The Wilammette Week*, (Portland, Oregon) Vol. 8, No. 12, 1982
3. Rajneesh, *The Book of the Secrets*, Vol. 1, Harper Colophon, 1977, p. 399
4. Ma Bharti, *The Ultimate Risk: Encountering Bhagwan Shree Rajneesh*, Evergreen Books, London, 1981, pp. 138–139 (In American Edition *Drunk on the Divine*, Grove Press, pp. 138–139
5. ibid, pp. 94–96
6. Interview *Sannyas*, May-June 1978, pp. 20–22

Chapter 23

1. Malachi Martin, *Hostage to the Devil*, Bantam, 1976, pp. 153–156
2. ibid, pp. 400–402
3. ibid, pp. 413–14
4. ibid, p. 432
5. ibid, pp. 469–70
6. ibid, pp. 482–83
7. ibid, p. 485
8. ibid, pp. 485–86

Chapter 25

1. Yarti, *The Sound of Running Water*, op. cit., p. 392
2. Justin Glass, *Witchcraft: The Sixth Sense*, Wilshire Books, 1974, p. 47
3. Richard Cavendish, *The Black Arts*, Putnam and Sons, p. 247

4. ibid, p. 48
5. ibid, p. 248
6. ibid, p. 249
7. Mircea Eliade, *Occultism, Witchcraft and Cultural Fashions*, University of Chicago, p. 71
8. See Mircea Eliade, *Yoga, Immortality, and Freedom*, University of Princeton, 1973, p. 305
9. ibid, p. 296
10. *Sannyas*, May-June 1979, p. 43
11. Doreen Valiente, *An ABC of Witchcraft*, St Martin's Press, p. 103

Nov 23, 1926 - birth

Mar. 8, 1940

Sai Baba 190

Eckart Flother

Hitler's obsessive occult prize, the
"spear of destiny" — pg 200

Also from Lion

Pilgrim's Guide to the New Age
Alice and Stephen Lawhead

A step-by-step tour of mysteries, philosophies, gurus and secrets
for the New Age explorer.

Once upon a time it was widely believed that science could (or
very soon would) expiain everything that went on in the
Universe. But then along came a few great unexplained things
like black holes, Adolf Hitler, extra-terrestrial sightings and
people who could bend spoons at will.

Since then, the human race, science, and the way we see
everything have changed for ever.

This book is a sightseer's guide for anyone journeying through
this brave new world. It charts the New Age beliefs that have
been imported from ancient China, or exported from present-
day California. It plots the 20th-century shock waves that have
been felt in the cinema, in the family home, in today's
architecture and on the psychiatrist's couch.

Pilgrim's Guide asks the big human questions. And it suggests
that answers can be found in the most unlikely places.

Illustrated in full colour

Lord of the Air – abridged
European version of *Avatar*
of Night by Tal Brooke
Robert Taliaferro Brooke